Critical University

Critical University

Moving Higher Education Forward

Tanya Loughead

Foreword by Peter McLaren

LEXINGTON BOOKS
Lanham • Boulder • New York • London

Published by Lexington Books
An imprint of The Rowman & Littlefield Publishing Group, Inc.
4501 Forbes Boulevard, Suite 200, Lanham, Maryland 20706
www.rowman.com

Unit A, Whitacre Mews, 26-34 Stannary Street, London SE11 4AB

British Library Cataloguing in Publication Information Available

Library of Congress Control Number: 2015950720
ISBN 978-0-7391-9375-4 (cloth : alk. paper)
ISBN 978-1-4985-2631-9 (electronic)

∞™ The paper used in this publication meets the minimum requirements of American National Standard for Information Sciences Permanence of Paper for Printed Library Materials, ANSI/NISO Z39.48-1992.

Printed in the United States of America

Contents

Foreword

Peter McLaren

The university has always been a contested site. But until the past half-century the forms and manners of contestation were mostly relegated to debates over how best to serve the public good and educate citizens to preserve what was still redeemable from American traditions and foster progressive social change. Today's captains of the corporate university would assuredly pause and perhaps snicker at such goals, if not wantonly abominating them from a business perspective as swathed in supine ignorance, then associating them with ancient history—perhaps the Lyceum of Athens populated by Aristotle and his peripatetic followers pacing back and forth in endless dialogue over the potentiality of matter. Over the past several decades alone, the political center of gravity has changed dramatically throughout campuses nationwide, so much so that the goal of *creating a critical citizenry* whose social responsibility is the deepening of democracy in all spheres of public life is now relegated to the odd syllabus posted on Facebook by "radical" educators in the humanities and social sciences and even at times in some colleges of education. In the 1980s, when I first started teaching in the academy, many of my colleagues agreed with me that the role of teaching critical citizenship was too conservative, that we needed to move beyond incremental reform and—following the advice of my mentor Paulo Freire—create multipolar sites, within the university, of popular democracy bolstered by pluriversity and interculturality. Today, even those tepid liberal initiatives of the 1980s seem a fundamental threat to the lifeblood of the modern university.

To any alert critic of the university who automatically recognizes that the production of knowledge is always a form of political action (Neary, 2012), the corporatization of the academy by "equity" specialists, venture capitalists, and hedge fund manipulators was visibly and irrevocably foreshadowed during the Reagan years when corporations amassed excessive power over the public sphere, initiating a moral panic surrounding the role of race, class, gender, and sexuality in required courses. At the same time this moral panic (in some ways a manufactured crisis) failed to address the attending trauma of the role played by neoliberal capitalism. The commodification of all official knowledge within the distorted legality of the state, and the spurious origin of all value production in the expropriation of the labor power of the worker (whether knowledge worker, cognitariat, or proletariat) is especially clear in an age of increasing fees and costs of education.

Universities are no longer democratizing institutions. The university operates more like a Civil War stockade or debtor's prison beholden to corporate managers whose market sovereignty has become the bulwark behind which neoliberal ideology can run amok on university campuses, masquerading as a necessary investment in training for new skill sets for the modern age fueled by a competitive global economy in which we are destined to function as lifelong learners. A new regime of accumulation known as cognitive capitalism appeared, with attendant new forms of cognitive labor that needed to be disciplined. Within the university, cognitive capitalism has become a new regime of accumulation, a training ground for capitalist cognitive labor where knowledge serves as the prime commodity (Neary, 2012). The prevailing marketized system of social development, the disappearance of shared governance—except as a corporate ruse—and the brutal conditions surrounding contingent workers (that has many part-time faculty dependent upon food stamps to survive) has turned universities into the *maquiladoras* of academic capitalism. Part-time faculty labor functions as a precariat sepulchered in a climate of servility and pressure.

The university is no longer being held accountable to society; it has become an instrument of divide and rule within the capitalist system. The normalizing gaze of the neoliberal academy treats knowledge as absolute, congealed and reified, in antiseptic isolation from the contextual specificity of its modes of production and social relations of distribution and consumption. For example, it is no longer a stage-whispered secret that the United States has become "the first genuine prison society in history" and the "world's largest jailor" (Street, 2001). This racism-induced spawning of over two million prison cells is now an integral part of a school-to-prison pipeline fertilized by white supremacy and the cash-nexus logic of what Street calls "correctional Keynesianism." In the words of singer-songwriter Leonard Cohen, "everybody knows" but unfortunately too few people in the academy are talking about it.

An historical reversal of the underground railroad or "freedom train" that became active after the Fugitive Slave Act of 1850, correctional Keynesianism has rapidly accelerated the growth of the prison population, and the result, as we all know (especially since Ferguson and Baltimore), has been a shockingly disproportionate African American and Latino inmate population. It should come as no surprise that the contemporary academy has played a determinative role in actively cultivating the conditions of possibility for the reproduction of the school-to-prison pipeline, evidenced by the renewed interest in prison labor all over the country.

Clearly, what is fueling the engine that powers neoliberal society today is the highly rationalized and individualized logic of private investment returns, evident in the priority our society places on prison construction and inmate containment over the social returns of a mobile, educated, and ethically informed critical citizenry. Markets today clearly have more freedom of movement than people. Draconian immigration laws keep the "outside other" behind the border and the frenzy of mass incarceration keeps the "inside other" behind bars. As a result, the belly of the prison population has begun to distend like a glutton on a binge from less than 180,000 in the early 1970s to over 2.3 million behind bars, and over 7.3 million in total in the correctional system by 2008. Over 70 percent of those currently in prison are people of color, though they make up only about 24 percent of the general population. Susan Searls Giroux (2015) has traced the events leading to California becoming home to the "largest prison building program in the history of the world" and garnering for the California Department of Corrections greater portions of the available state appropriations, and prompting waves of critical studies by the state's universities. She notes, however, that the university egregiously failed to challenge the political exploitation of an electorate whose fears of crime were fueled by ever-increasing media reportage, even in periods when crime rates stabilized or fell. In other words, the academy in the main was hit with a suffocating social amnesia and an ineluctable failure of nerve in failing to raise ethical or philosophical questions about the shifting nature of incarceration from "rehabilitation" to "punishment" (Giroux, in press). Furthermore, it neglected to raise necessary sociological or criminological questions about the social production of crime, the worrisome attributes of the carceral society, or increasing rates of poor and minority youth behind bars. Rather, what resulted was the "pitched competition" between the California Department of Corrections and all other state agencies dependent on the general fund. What the university did provide, however, was appalling: assistance in managing the rationalized logic of cost effectiveness and "efficiency expertise" in helping prisons reduce the costs of its burgeoning incarcerated populations. Of course, in 1995, the Regents of the University of California famously recognized that affirmative action was "an inefficient (nonmarket) mode of resource allocation" and shed this policy over the objections of faculty and staff (Gilmore, 2007). Community colleges jumped into the fray, offering training programs for police and prison guards; courses in specialized forensics and associate degrees in correctional science flourished (Gilmore, 2007; Giroux, in press).

University critics such as Susan Searls Giroux, Henry Giroux (both of McMaster University in Canada) and Mike Neary (of the University of Lincoln in England) have emphasized the important roles of professors as insurgent and public intellectuals. Neary, for instance, has urged professors and students to participate in the creation of a new university grounded in a radical political project based on the practices of self-education and militant co-research. Asserting that education as a whole needs to be reinvented as a revolutionary political project, Neary emphasizes the urgency of challenging the enterprise business culture that has infected the academy and institutionalizing the university as a model of democratic governance as well as a communal site for the struggle for social justice. In an age of neoliberal capitalism, this task is no easy matter. My own work (in press) questions whether or not the university can be salvaged as long as it is situated in the larger social universe of value production (I am using *value* here in the Marxist sense of value as determined by socially necessary labor time, which is the central abstraction that dominates life under capitalism). I am further questioning how the role of the university can be made more compatible with Marx's definition of revolutionary practice as the "coincidence of the changing of circumstances and of human activity or self-changing" by reengineering the relationship between mental and manual labor (Marx, 1970). After all, it is this coincidence of social transformation and transformation of consciousness which is likely to provide the kind of militant public engagement necessary to transform social relations of capitalist exploitation both outside of the university as well as within it. The role of the university will be more clearly discerned in in periods of heightened class struggle and revolution, and unless such struggle is successful, we cannot know in detail the contours of the alternative, and it is precisely in public spheres such as the university where we hope that some of those details and plans for action can emerge. The point that I am making here is that the task of reshaping the university is dialectically related to the task of building the alternative to capitalist value production. As we challenge capitalism at its roots, a detailed new role for the university will emerge, a role that can help us transition to a socialist alternative to capitalism (McLaren, in press).

Here it is important to recall the militant history of Paris 8, bulldozed in 1980 and moved out of Paris to the suburbs of St. Denis, a victim of its own success in radicalizing students (Neary, 2012). In a similar vein, we can look to the important work of The Edu-Factory Collective and Autonomous Education Network in our attempt to reclaim the commons. In so doing we can appreciate the mercurial arguments and demands put forward by groups such as the University of Utopia, the All Nepal National Free Student Union, the Carrott Workers Collective, Critical Legal Thinking, Direct Action from Ukraine, the Slow University of Warsaw, Fakultat Null from Berlin, the Pan Africa Student Council from Gambia, the Street University of Russia,

Öğrenci Kolektifleri from Turkey, the Association of the Blacklisted Students of Tokyo, and Upping The Anti from Canada (Neary, 2011), some of whom have collectivized to form a type of "undercommons" under the title, The Knowledge Liberation Front.

It is in the context of the above efforts at transforming the university in the service of helping others discover a meaningful life and liberating the university from its current activity in the reproduction of civic cowardice and technocratic rationality that the work of Tanya Loughead becomes so important. In this brilliant book, *Critical University*, Loughead immediately recognizes that in the face of today's austerity capitalism, specific forms of liberatory political subjectivity need to be developed by and among students and educators in university settings. In this way she does not bewail the present state of the academy as much as function as a warrior of critical consciousness, dedicated to creating "liberating persons and societies" with one of her strongest weapons—philosophy—that she wields like a mighty broadsword, clearing pathways in what she calls "freedom-work" that enable students and teachers alike to *be free with others* in order to *promote freedom for others* by creating the multifaceted contexts for students and colleagues to liberate themselves by reading simultaneously both the word and the world. Her book is not about self-fashioning within the current crisis of identity made fashionable by some of the apostates of poststructuralism; rather, it is about self and social transformation and as such is irredeemably dialectical, focusing on the cultivation of a radical aesthetics redolent of the work of the later Marcuse and adapted toward creating a revolutionary praxis.

Loughead's critical pedagogy—that draws upon the work of Paulo Freire, bell hooks, and other critical educators—is fashioned out of a philosophy of praxis, directed toward a "rebirthing" of the social as well as the self, an internalizing of the external and an externalizing of the internal, in order to *create pedagogical differences that make a difference.* Here, Loughead's work echoes surrealism's attempt to *make the strange familiar and the familiar strange.* Clearly, Loughead understands that you can't teach anybody anything, as the late Myles Horton once said, you can only create contexts where people can learn. Approaching her subject from a multidisciplinary perspective, in which a range of strategies of disruption are brought to bear on the question of what constitutes critical knowledge and the purposes served by such knowledge (i.e., asking questions about what knowledge is of most worth in the university and whose interests are served by such knowledge), Loughead teaches us the importance of breaking free of our assigned roles in the transnational workplace and to "re-volt" our subjective selves and in the process create radically sufficient protagonistic agency to—put simply—change the world. These protagonistic actions against the neoliberal hegemonic structures and institutions of cognitive capitalism utilize forms of counterpower that can be conscripted into the purpose of creating a larger counterpublic sphere.

Putting into practice a confluence of radical philosophical perspectives—Althusserian, Foucauldian, Derridean, Freirean, Marcusean, Kristevean, Husserlian and more—surrounding how knowledge is produced and valued, and under what conditions it is utilized and for what purposes, Loughead puts under a hermeneutics of suspicion *the financialization and alienation of everyday life*, including normativized and accepted institutional arrangements, epistemologies supporting a coloniality of power, established cultural formations, social relations of production, structured hierarchies of race, class, gender and sexuality, regnant discourses and practices of ableism, speciesism, and goals and purposes of education that are part of both the manifest and hidden curriculum of the corporate university. Loughead recognizes only too well that conscientization (Freire's term) is not achieved by hurling the lightning bolt of critical consciousness into the bewildered herd below, but by charting critical vectors within geometries of insurgency: spaces that are nonhierarchical, democratic and self-organized that provide the means for students to become critically literate and to be able to act with clarity and coherence in the service of creating a living knowledge for the public good.

Written with verve, cultivation, and grittiness, *Critical University* is a powerful contribution to the field of critical university studies as well as critical pedagogy. What is striking about Loughead's personal investment in (what she calls) freedom-work is her active refusal to separate *theory from practice, head from heart, action from reflection* and her unwillingness to adapt students to an insane world of pain and privation. Her passionate commitment to both a language of critique and praxis of possibility enables her students and colleagues the opportunity to live as agents and makers of history rather than as uncritical servants of history. In teaching against the grain, Loughead fundamentally adheres to a pedagogy of endogenous development, believing it to be as important as transforming the social relations of capitalist production. In a dialectical fashion she approaches her pedagogy of liberation by emphasizing the twin roles of reform and revolution. Underscoring the role of dialectics as a form of mediation and not juxtaposition, Loughead does not posit the false choice of either reform or revolution. Rather, she assumes the position that *both* reform and revolution matter. Hers is a pedagogy in the subjunctive mode: We do what we can within the contextual specificity of where we find ourselves yet always holding to a vision of what the future could be. Such a vision is never static but always in the making. Taking the lived experiences of her students as a starting point, Loughead understands that experiences are never transparent but are always populated by accumulated historical meanings and interpretations that need to be unpacked, interrogated critically and, if necessary, transformed in the interests of the greater good of society. *Critical University* provides the lineaments of such a vision. We will not only become better educators as a result of critically engaging Loughead's vision, but better agents of history.

REFERENCES

Giroux, Henry. (2015). "Higher Education and the Promise of Insurgent Public Memory," http://truth-out.org/news/item/29396-higher-education-and-the-promise-of-insurgent-public-memory

Giroux, Susan Searls. (In press). *Between Race and Reason: Violence, Intellectual Responsibility, and the University to Come*. Stanford, CA: Stanford University Press.

Neary, Michael. (2012) "Teaching politically: policy, pedagogy and the new European university." http://eprints.lincoln.ac.uk/6510 *Journal for Critical Education Policy Studies*, 10(2). 233–257.

Marx, Karl. "These on Feuerbach," in *The German Ideology*. London: Lawrence and Wishart, 1970.

McLaren, Peter. (In press). *Pedagogy of Insurrection: From Resurrection to Revolution*. New York: Peter Lang Publishers.

Street, Paul. "Race, Prison, and Poverty: The Race to Incarcerate in *The Age of Correctional Keynesianism*." *Z Magazine*, May 2001, 25–31. http://www.zcommunications.org/race-prison-and-poverty-by-paul-street.

Gilmore, Ruth Wilson. "Golden Gulag: Prisons, Surplus, Crisis, and Opposition in *Globalizing California*." Berkeley, CA: University of California Press, 2007.

Acknowledgments

"Phenomenology demands . . . [that one be] a humble worker in community with others." —Husserl

Gratitude seems always an issue of memory, for certainly none of us could have the ideas that we have—let alone the time, the material conditions, or confidence to express them—without every person, place, book, artwork, party, encounter, relationship, every support and every slight, every love and every frustration, both conscious and unconscious. (Nietzsche questions whether Epicurus philosophized out of malice aimed at Plato; whether Spinoza's ethics stem from unconscious vengefulness.)

When we rightly recognize that we are whatever provocations surround us—we can only further seek and soak up those life forces and hope to provoke others in life affirmation as gratitude. Teaching and activism are my acts of gratitude.

That said, for this particular project, I must mention first of all Jasmina Tacheva, my former student, research assistant, and spirited conversationalist, poet, and philosopher. We both have so much to say (and all at once!) that words and thoughts seem to manifest in the air between us. I thank Hunter Dudkiewicz, another former student: we read Althusser, Žižek and Hegel together, comrades in delight. I thank *all* of my students at Canisius College. I thank my colleagues in the Department of Philosophy. I thank fellow Buffalo activists. I also thank many friends who surround me with discussion, contradiction, and fresh ideas including Alexander Bertland, George Boger, Jon DiCicco, Ami Lake, Joshua Mills-Knutsen, Patrick Murray, Anthony Nocella, Gail Presbey, and many Facebook friends with whom to spar and float ideas. No one's ideas come fully formed—all are in formation dialectically with and against others.

I thank Canisius College for two research grants and a sabbatical that helped in the creation of this book. I am a philosophy professor with tenure at a small liberal arts Jesuit school with a mission for social justice. I benefit from institutional and mission-centric support.

I most heartily thank Peter McLaren for his foreword, but also more broadly for the *communal spirit* with which he undertakes intellectual work.

Finally: Girish, what exhilaration to be with you conversing, arguing, laughing, loving, viewing, dialecting, and learning—trying to figure out the aesthetic and political shape of the world. Where things seem to have gone flat, let's be a part of analyzing and fixing that shit!

I thank all of you who pick up this book, whether you do so out of boredom or fascination, optimism or pessimism, whether you are a friend, enemy, student, administrator, citizen, or philosopher: Let's think together.

Chapter One

Raising an Eyebrow at the University

Anxiety and foreboding mark the state of higher education today. This is especially so for those of us who work in the humanities, who are contingent workers, and/or those of us who believe in the critical potential of education. Even the old Enlightenment notion of education—as a force for freeing the mind from false authorities, for scientific ways of knowing, for promoting intellectual courage and curiosity—seems too idealistic a vision in the current age. A naïve dreamer who holds such ideals is told this: Be realistic! Get with the program! How can you think of such luxuries in our economically straitened times?

Imagine this: Late afternoon. Students under a sun-dappled oak tree, absorbed in Shakespeare. A backdrop of majestic, ivy-caressed stone buildings. Tenured professors in tweed jackets with elbow patches, tomes under their arm, strolling to the dean's suite to gather, sip sherry, share stories and a few warm laughs. What a *charming* image!

This picture of academia as enchanting but not quite in step with—not *useful* enough—for the contemporary age is one that cries out for deconstruction. Many current defenses of the university fall into a traditionalist nostalgia: they want to "conserve" the university of old. But that is not the position of this work. For those of us who believe in the critical potential of higher education, there *is* something worth conserving about traditional higher education and it's not necessarily the oak tree or the sherry or even the Shakespeare. Instead, it is an openness and a critical, reflective deportment to the world. The university must have one eyebrow raised. The world must forever remain a question: true scholars in every field know this.

This very openness that should constitute the deportment of the university is—as many are warning—under threat. The openness of inquiry (the only way to be truly scholarly) has been narrowed in ways that many deem the *corporatization of the university*. To fight for the scholarly meaning of the university nowadays is to be a radical. The corporatization affects some of us more than others (though, to clarify, I care less about how it affects us as individuals in particular fields and more about how it affects the world, though certainly the two are related). We cannot do our work as critical scholars and teachers of (for instance) feminism, critical history, or environmental justice if students are not signing up for our courses because they are not a part of robust general education requirements, or if our positions, departments, or schools no longer exist. Worse so if we are contingent or adjunct labor who work for much less pay, little to no benefits, and the constant threat that our courses or positions may be cut if they are not "popular" with administration, full-time professors, and/or students. In the United States, the number of courses taught by contingent professors now exceeds the number of courses taught by full-time faculty members.[1] And at the same time that we shrink the number and the power of full-time faculty, we grow the middle-management of universities. Critical education—the openness of inquiry—becomes increasingly difficult in this setting.

Most of us believe that education is a social good; thus a threat to robust and critical education is a threat to society in general. What are the real and present dangers? Broadly speaking, we face budget cuts and fights over how dwindling funds should be allocated; the cutting of liberal arts requirements in core curricula across the nation; the closing or redefinition of liberal arts colleges; the narrowing of what gets defined as "education" to only career preparation; traditionally tenure-track positions being filled by adjuncts and other contingent faculty; the emphasis that "successful" departments and professors are those who get private grants from corporations; the growing emphasis on short-term assessment geared toward an instrumentalist view of education; and the shifting of leadership positions at universities from academics to business, law, or administrative professionals who have little (or no) experience as teacher-scholars in universities.

Let's take a closer look at some of the ways in which the corporatization of the university threatens critical education in particular. To focus our inquiry, I propose that it occurs in six key ways:

1. the weakening of shared governance;
2. the increase of administration and decrease in full-time faculty;
3. the increasing importance of grants;
4. the lack of importance given to teaching;
5. the waning importance of the humanities to undergraduate education; and
6. the rising commodification and cost of higher education in the United States.

SHARED GOVERNANCE

Cary Nelson, former president of the American Association of University Professors, believes that the number one threat against universities providing critical education is a lack of shared governance. He writes,

> Of course the aim of preparing students to be critical participants in a democracy . . . is exactly what the corporate university typically seeks to undermine. Faculty members' academic freedom gives them the right to shape instruction so as to enhance students' ability to be critical citizens . . . [but] corporatized universities oriented toward income generation and job training had already begun opting instead for strictly instrumental instructional aims. . . . therefore, unless shared governance includes a faculty role in defining institutional mission, everything else about the educational environment is at risk.[2]

In his detailed history of the American university, Larry G. Gerber argues that it is thanks to shared governance and a professionalized faculty that American universities gained prestige and influence in the second half of the twentieth century.[3]

On the other hand, Henry Rosovsky writes that faculty have always seen themselves—not as "employees" of a university—but as owners in a cooperative venture of education.[4] However, his description of a professor reflects a previous era—an era when almost all professors were tenured and when administration came from the ranks of tenured professors. In fact, his book was published in 1990, and so it tells much about the changes that have occurred between 1990 and 2010 when we compare the positions of Rosovsky (1990) and Nelson (2010). Rosovsky writes, "We professors have the income of civil servants but the freedom of artists," and "[t]his imposes certain obligations. The formal duties imposed by our institutions are minimal. . . . Yet most of us work long hours. . . . We do our profession as a calling, considering ourselves not employees but shareholders of the university: a group of owners."[5] What Rosovsky does not know that Nelson does is that this "shareholder/owner" status needs to be constantly and consistently defended. It is not a given, nor has it ever been. In order for the entire campus (faculty, students, staff, administrators and boards of trustees) to believe and act upon the notion that 'we are all in this together as mutual shareholders' there has to be respect and a shared vision of the purposes and meanings of higher education. With the growing corporatization of higher education, with administrators and boards of trustees coming more and more from the corporate world (and not academia), there is the real possibility that this "shareholder" status is just a charming image or patronizing invitation to offer an opinion to the bosses (an "opinion" that may or may not be acted upon by administration), but not a real share in the mission and management of the university.

The Yeshiva court case famously states that many private colleges cannot unionize precisely because faculty are a part of management. [6] Gerber writes, "In a five-to-four opinion, the court held that full-time faculty members at Yeshiva University were excluded from coverage by the National Labor Relations Act by virtue of their being 'managerial employees' who were 'involved in developing and enforcing employer policy.'" He quotes the majority opinion of the Yeshiva case "arguing that the authority of the faculty 'in academic matters is absolute,'" including all courses, scheduling of courses, who teaches them and to whom they will be taught, all grading standards, teaching methods, faculty hiring, tenure and promotion, and furthermore faculty has power even "beyond strictly academic concerns."[7] That court case reflects the image that Rosovsky wrote about. Let us also remember that it is true that *tenured faculty* do have a lot of choices in how they spend their time—it is possible to keep one's job doing minimal work. But, we are still only talking about less than 30 percent of the professors on campus (70 percent of courses in higher education are taught by contingent labor).[8] The less that the faculty has control over academics, the more instrumental (and less critical) that education becomes.

A more recent case puts the Yeshiva case into question. In the Pacific Lutheran University case ruling of December 2014, the court "rejected the claims of Pacific Lutheran University that its full-time, non-tenure track faculty members are managerial employees and thus are not entitled to collective bargaining."[9]

> Indeed, our experience applying Yeshiva has generally shown that colleges and universities are increasingly run by administrators, which has the effect of concentrating and centering authority away from the faculty in a way that was contemplated in Yeshiva, but found not to exist at Yeshiva University itself. Such considerations are relevant to our assessment of whether the faculty constitute managerial employees. A common manifestation of this 'corporatization' of higher education that is specifically relevant to the faculty in issue here is the use of 'contingent faculty,' that is, faculty who, unlike traditional faculty, have been appointed with no prospect of tenure and often no guarantee of employment beyond the academic year.[10]

Inside Higher Ed calls the National Labor Relations Board (NLRB) ruling a "win" since now unionization will be much easier at private colleges. I am unsure. On the one hand, of course unionization is positive in that in challenges the power at the top of a hierarchy with the power of numbers at the bottom of the hierarchy. Unionization is a force for more democratic decision making—decision making that tends to favor interests of the many instead of the few. This is all good. Also, the ruling seems a correct ruling that faculty are not treated as managers in the current day by most colleges. On the other hand, I'm not sure that faculty having a union in and of itself will fix all (or perhaps even most) of the problems that faculty truly being treated as managers (as the original Yeshiva case attested to) does. It remains to be seen. Faculty will have to commit themselves to the service of shared governance in a broad way. Let us hope that if and when faculty form unions that we do not focus narrowly on the pay and benefits of tenured and tenure-track faculty. This should be the last item on the list of concerns of corporatized higher education. Having a greater stake in all college decisions (i.e., shared governance) is much more important and should be at the top of our list of concerns. True "managers" will have a meaningful voice in all aspects of the university. They will not be merely "consultative" by making "recommendations"—they will be shared decision makers in the future of the university. One of Paulo Freire's criticisms of Leninist strains of Marxism is that it stresses economic justice—but Stanley Aronowitz rightly points out that economic justice might conceivably be reached "without shared decision-making." [11] For this reason, "Freire *defines* class consciousness as the power and the will" to "*share* in the formulation of the conditions of knowledge and futurity." [12] Giving up on having a meaningful voice on administrative hires, tenure and promotion guidelines, hiring choices, building acquisition decisions, budgeting, academic standards, program review, mission statements, institutional planning and more all for better pay and benefits package is a Faustian trade we shouldn't accept.

GROWTH IN ADMINISTRATION/ DECREASE OF FULL-TIME FACULTY

When we talk about the financial problems at many contemporary colleges and universities, we often talk in terms of bringing in new revenue and/or cutting expenditures. But there is another option worth discussing: we can *rearrange* the monies that are available in a way that is in keeping with the highest virtues of higher education. A rearrangement has been occurring over the past thirty years, but it is not in keeping with what works best for our students' education. The proportion of resources allocated to administration, staff and athletics has been creeping up—rapidly—and the overall amount of money spent on teaching has been going down. As Benjamin Ginsberg observes, between 1975 and 2005, total spending by American universities tripled, to more than \$325 billion per year. [13]

> Over the same period, the faculty-to-student ratio has remained fairly constant, at approximately fifteen or sixteen students per instructor. One thing that has changed, dramatically, is the administrator-per-student ratio. In 1975, colleges employed one administrator for every eighty-four students and one professional staffer—admissions officers, information technology specialists, and the like—for every fifty students. By 2005, the administrator-to-student ratio had

dropped to one administrator for every sixty-eight students while the ratio of professional staffers had dropped to one for every twenty-one students.[14]

In the last twenty-five years, the number of nonacademic administrative and professional staff at American colleges and universities has doubled, and inflation-adjusted spending on administration per student increased by 61 percent.[15] Administrative/managerial staff has increased 44.6 percent between 1999 and 2009.[16] A 2012 study conducted by economists Robert E. Martin and R. Carter Hill states that presently, administrators outnumber full-time faculty with two full-time administrators for every one tenured or tenure-track faculty member.[17] The same study concludes however, that the optimal (i.e., most cost-effective) ratio of tenure-track faculty to administrators is 3:1.[18] In an article for *The Chronicle of Higher Education,* Martin notes that, "Reason and data alike suggest that the largest part of the problem is that it is administrators and members of governing boards who have too much influence over how resources are used."[19] He refers to the parallel processes of the declining influence tenure-track faculty on one hand, and the proliferation of non-academic professional staff on the other, as "bureaucratic entropy," and argues that, "In academe, shared governance is the only natural constraint on the pursuit of self-interest."[20] Without it, the mechanism of checks and balances in higher education runs the risk of breaking down. "The balance between people who are actually in the trenches and those who are overseeing that work has gotten grossly out of line. . . . That imbalance is one of the primary reasons for why costs grew so out of control over the last three years," Martin says in another article.[21] A 2011 study conducted by the Service Employees International Union found the average employee to manager ratio in the largest state agencies (with at least 1,000 employees) to be 6.1-to-1, and 4.6-to-1 in smaller agencies. In the private sector, a similar situation can be observed: a report by the U.S. Merit Systems Protection Board shows an increase in the number of managers and supervisors, constituting 14.6 percent of the total employee workforce in 2008.[22] We should note that this movement toward more administration and fewer workers is not limited to academia. In 1950, there were ten workers for every one manager; in 2010, the ratio is three workers to every one administrator.

According to *Labor Intensive or Labor Expensive? Changing Staffing and Compensation Patterns in Higher Education,* a report from the Delta Cost Project database, "Faculty salaries were not the leading cause of rising college tuitions during the past decade. Increased benefits costs, nonfaculty positions added elsewhere on campus, declines in state and institutional subsidies, and other factors all played a role. The average salary outlay per full-time faculty member has stayed essentially flat from 2002 to 2010." "Institutions have continued to hire full-time faculty, but at a pace that either equaled or lagged behind student enrollments; these new hires also were likely to fill non-tenure-track positions." For more than a decade, colleges and universities have tried to manage costs by increasingly relying on part-time instructors.[23] By way of example, at my own college, we created more vice presidential positions[24] during the same time that we threatened the positions of eight tenure-track faculty.[25] At our local community college, during the same year that tuition went up $300 for students and that there was a freeze on hiring full-time faculty (and of course a reliance upon underpaid adjuncts), that college invented a new administrative position at the vice presidential level for a former politician. Luckily, that story made it into the paper and created a stir.[26]

When more slices of the pie go to upper administration, less is "left over" to serve the educational function of the school. Increasingly, we leave the adjuncts to take care of that. According to Noam Chomsky, this is perfectly analogous to Wal-Mart choosing to hire cheap, expendable labor with no benefits. "It's a part of a corporate business model designed to reduce labor costs and to increase labor servility."[27] This creates a class of workers that Chomsky calls the "precariat"—those with little to no rights, economic stability, academic freedom, or voice in the university. The precariat is in the perfect spot for an administrative sector that wants to "keep costs down and make sure that labor is docile and obedient."[28] One problem is that while faculty may be in danger of losing their jobs if they don't please the administrators, the administrators are under no such threat. Furthermore, administration is increasingly composed of an entirely separate class of individuals who do not come from the faculty—such persons have no experience as teacher-scholars and therefore do not genuinely grasp the mission and purposes of higher education. "There are more and more professional administrators, layer after layer of them, with more and more positions being taken remote from the faculty controls."[29]

Many wonder why and how this is occurring. One reason (as mentioned earlier) is that faculty have little influence on administrative search committees. This goes back to our earlier discussion about shared governance—when there are faculty on search committees, their numbers are usually low, and in many cases, these positions are created and filled without faculty input, which puts the whole Yeshiva ruling (that faculty are part of management) into question. We have all heard about the astronomical paychecks of some university presidents, many in the millions per year. The ten highest-paid private-college presidents cost their institutions an average of about $2.3-million each in 2011.[30] According to *The Chronicle of Higher Education*, forty-two college presidents received salaries of more than $1,000,000 in 2011, compared to thirty-six a year earlier.[31] *The Chronicle* also points out that the number of presidents who have crossed the million-dollar threshold is not limited to private universities: Four public-college presidents made more than \$1-million in 2011–2012, up from three the previous year.[32]

The defense given in the corporate world is that an organization must offer this kind of "compensation package" in order to attract the best candidates. I've heard the same market-based reasoning given for why universities must offer high salaries for top administrators. This rationale is dubious: first, the meaning of "best" is far from clear. Typically what corporations (and increasingly, universities) mean is that they want someone who has been in top management at another corporation. Or in the case of the University of Texas, they might accept someone who has leadership experience in the military: In July 2014, the Board of Regents of The University of Texas System voted unanimously to name Adm. William H. McRaven—a man who has no PhD and no experience as a teacher-scholar, as the sole finalist for the job of chancellor to oversee fifteen campuses and \$14 billion budget.[33] There is little data that this kind of rationale (the more you pay, the better leadership candidates you attract) works for universities. Further, when paying this kind of money takes away from resources we can devote to the classroom, it is completely reasonable that we would want data to assure us that our money will be well spent. (This is the case even if we remain within the realm of *market-based reasoning* and do not raise ethical or educational challenges to these compensation packages.) But we find no such assurance. In fact, back in the day (say, fifty years ago), when administrators were paid only marginally more than full professors and when all administrators came out of the ranks of the professorship, universities as a group were more stable, held down tuition costs, and (somehow!) had funds available for more full-time teachers in the classroom. No doubt this is an overdetermined case and there are many causes to the current crises in higher education, but I only list this data to show that giving our top administrators high "compensation packages" is not making our colleges and universities stronger, more stable, or more affordable for our students. In my mind there is simply no rational justification for them. Moreover, in the case of the public university, it is not clear *why* the public should support any college or university with rampant levels of inequality and such poor concern for what is best *for students* and for serving the public good. Public funds should serve the public good and it's extremely unclear that million dollar presidents, football teams, or splashy PR campaigns do so.

We must also make mention of the assessment culture that has swept across college and university campuses in the United States. Most faculty see assessment as a necessary evil. Accrediting boards—in my own case the Middle States Association of Colleges and Schools, but others include Northwest, North Central, Southern, Western, and New England—hand down dictums of what student learning assessment should look like and claim that if we don't prove that student learning is occurring, then we do not deserve to be an accredited university. In principle, I agree with this. Of course, all committed faculty want to believe that our students are learning in our courses. And surely we all want to live in a society where we can be sure that a college degree has strong educational merit regardless of which institution it came from. So, the problem is not the accrediting board itself, not the *what* or *why* of it, but the *how*. Imagine an accrediting board that required (for instance) that a college or university be structured such that a minimum of 85 percent of courses in every department be taught by full-time, qualified professors with terminal degrees in their fields. The quality of education for our students would surely rise. Imagine that an accrediting board stipulated that no full-time worker (including administrators) may earn more than four times the salary of the lowest-paid full-time worker on campus? (So that if, for instance, a maintenance worker makes $50,000 per year, that a president could not make more than $200,000 per year.) That would also lead to a rise in the quality of our institutions because those becoming administrators would do so more due to a sense of mission and dedication to the task, rather than doing so for a fatter paycheck or a rise in status. I am reminded of Socrates' words that the good society would make no one a leader who wanted to lead on the basis of honor or money. A good leader will not want to lead at all, but will do so out of a sense of wisdom and fit for the position.[34] Imagine also that accrediting boards stipulated class size and full-time professor to student ratios. All students could expect to be in, for instance, classes of thirty or less, with a committed full-time and qualified professor in the room. Again, a huge escalation in the quality and meaning of our college experience would occur. Accrediting boards may be—at this point in history—a set of organizations with enough power to change the administration-faculty power dynamic that has arisen in the past decades. In short, I can imagine that university-accrediting boards could be a force for good in society, faithfully serving the public good. But they are not now. It is important to look at their work because accrediting boards are a field of power that top administrators pay attention to and thus contain a possible strategy for altering the system (in addition, of course, to tenured faculty, students, unions, workers and the general public demanding more from our centers of higher education).

GRANTS CULTURE

Next let us talk about the increasing emphasis upon departments and professors to win outside grants. Robert Jensen from the University of Texas at Austin tells a story about going to a faculty meeting where the dean announced unilaterally that obtaining grants was now a required part of getting tenure and promotion: "The ability to raise money, up to that point, had never been explicitly listed as a requirement, and many of us who had been tenured in the past years had not been expected to raise money."[35] Jensen rightly notes that not all fields have equal access to private funding and that in most fields, what funding there is available requires one to defend *status quo* perspectives. For instance, in the sciences, there may be "money available for research that is not overtly tied to ideological positions" but in other fields, "especially certain disciplines in the humanities and social sciences, funding is harder to come by and more overtly ideological in character."[36] Jensen notes that in his field of journalism, the major funders are connected to the industry and they "have never funded critical research that might lead to conclusions in conflict with their interests."[37] Therefore, the logical question becomes this: "Given that the sources of funding for scholars doing critical research are considerably fewer than for those doing research that accepts the existing system, isn't this demand on faculty, in fact, going to result in less critical research?"[38] Jensen's dean presented this new requirement for tenure and promotion as an allegedly "neutral rule" since "Everyone who goes up for tenure or promotion faces the same expectations,"[39] but obviously this is *not* a neutral rule since private funding is not available (1) to all fields equally, and (2) to persons who do research that may critique systems of power and capital. As Baez and Boyles point out, in these cases it seems that "the tenure system is now serving the imperatives of the corporate culture."[40] "It is the capitalists who will attain tenure" since "faculty who do the bulk of the teaching—the 'mere' teachers—are increasingly those with no tenure."[41]

So there are at least two problems with requiring grants for promotion and tenure. The first problem is this system often undermines the academic standard that specialists in a field are those best positioned to make claims about what counts as strong scholarship within a field. A grants culture gives that power to administrators and to outside forces, rather than to one's peers in the field. In Jensen's story, this rule requiring grants was instituted in a hierarchical corporate manner from the dean—not a requirement decided upon jointly by faculty who, after all, are the experts on what counts as good scholarship and research (earlier in his piece he writes that at University of Texas, shared governance is window-dressing, "there is no faculty governance and all committees are merely consultative"[42]). The second problem is that ultimately this will lead to universities becoming less and less critical or questioning of the society around them. Indeed, those who rise in the ranks and in the prestige that large grants confer will most likely be the defenders of *status quo* ideology, and not those who raise critical and ethical questions. The result is that the university becomes the polar *opposite* of what it should be. The university should be a space in society where open-minded and questioning scholars pose critical questions. This cannot and will not occur in a higher education system that requires grants.

It is worth noting that in Jensen's story, the faculty the University of Texas did not raise serious concerns with the dean on this unilateral change on the tenure and promotion requirements. For that, Jensen rightly blames the faculty: "What was more disturbing was the reaction of my faculty colleagues . . . full professors, some with endowed chairs and professorships— chose to remain silent. . . . That's a well-disciplined class." [43] These shifts in the corporatization of academia are usually blamed on administration and boards of trustees, but Jensen and I agree that the tenured faculty are equally to blame. As Henry Giroux notes,

> intellectuals often exist in hermetic academic bubbles cut off from both the larger public and the important issues that impact society. To no small degree, they have been complicit in the transformation of the university into an adjunct of corporate and military power. [44]

I take but one example here. The documentary film *The Future of Food*[45] investigates the increasing power and influence that large corporations (in particular Monsanto) have over our food system—power over us as both farmers and consumers, "every link in the chain of food production is being dominated by fewer and fewer large corporations." [46] There are several dangers to this approach including (1) the lack of diversity in crops; if a disease were to wipe out the predominant type of corn grown in the United States, we would have little to fall back upon, and a food crisis would be likely; (2) farmers of some crops are no longer self-sufficient as they are forced to buy their seeds (and herbicides) from Monsanto and suffer lawsuits if they don't but their own crops are accidentally pollinated from Monsanto's seeds; (3) the safety and health of genetically modified crops has not been fully tested and many—including many national governments—claim that they may be dangerous[47]; (4) many ethical questions arise about the private ownership and patenting of life forms (Vandana Shiva writes about this[48]); (5) money and control flows to the north (to corporations in the United States) from the south (increasing the global inequality gap) as more of the Third World loses the rights and/or ability to plant the grains and food that they have been growing for centuries; (6) when a few large companies have so much power, they are increasingly able to control the market and government policy; and (7) increasingly have control over university research. While all of these issues warrant serious questioning, it is number seven that interests us here. Many scientists compete for grants to do research that ultimately serves the interests of companies like Monsanto. This means that we—in not-for-profit centers of higher education devised to serve the public good—are also partly responsible for those other six dangers listed above. This is also the perfect illustration of how universities can work against critical thinking. Some scientists claim that we are seeing a narrowing down of research in the field of biology in particular.[49] They claim that those professors and researchers who "go with the ideological flow" of promoting popular and lucrative businesses are rewarded handsomely for their compliance. Those who choose to question that flow get little to no grant money. Ignacio Chapela says that his research study on crop diversification at Berkeley was run on $2,000, "compare that with the $25 million coming the other way" from biotech industry supporting GMOs in Berkeley alone.[50] There is "small tolerance" for those who "directly challenge" the industry status quo.[51] What occurs is that along with a lack of "genetic diversity," there is also a lack of "intellectual diversity."[52]

In *The Politics of Inquiry*, Baez and Boyles question certain assumptions about what makes an "excellent" university by questioning the grants culture. They claim that there is no data proving that more research makes for better teaching. In fact, professors often use higher research obligations as a way to escape teaching—for instance using their grant money to "buy" themselves out of teaching. Even at a liberal arts teaching college like mine, we have professors who—instead of teaching the three courses per semester that is the norm—teach only one course per semester. At so-called "research 1" schools, it is even more common to see the equation, greater research = less teaching. So the claim that professors should do more research in order to be better teachers in the classroom is dubious logic.

A common belief about grants is that they free the professor from the authority of the university and its demands, that a professor with grant money has more freedom and autonomy. But is that really true, or has one merely substituted one power structure for another? Who wields power and authority over the work of faculty? Who gets to decide the worth of faculty scholarship? Without grants, authority lies with the university as a whole—the faculty and administration with whom you work, along with peers in your field. With grants, authority lies with the corporation or organization that awards your grant money. In neither case is the professor totally "free" to do as he or she wants—but his or her university is likely to be (or should be) open to more kinds of research that aren't necessarily directly "useful" to the capitalist economy and its private corporations. We should also ask a Foucauldian question here—sure, some research gets funded, but what about the questions that never get asked, what about the formulation of the research questions themselves? In a grants culture, won't professors only ask questions that have a likelihood of getting funded, and thus be instrumental in nature? This is not the supposed "open" questioning of scholars that I stated at the start of this chapter was the purpose of the university. Baez and Boyles, by the way, are not just pointing the finger at greedy capitalists and administrators here—they lay the blame on faculty members themselves.

A broader, more philosophical point needs to be raised concerning the growing use of grants. As long as universities have existed there has been

both the implicit and explicit expectation that they serve the common good—
the public. This is partly the rationale behind universities being granted "not-
for-profit" status: *education serves the public good*. Those who defend the
use of grants claim that they are a part of this long history of service: using
university labor, labs, knowledge, and power in order to serve forces outside
the university (i.e., "the public"). What needs philosophical analysis is the
manner in which the word *public* is being used. Grants redefine "public" to
mean a private organization, a corporate or military interest—not the common good. We have to be clear about this because it is not the case that
everything outside the gates of the university = the public good. We have to
ask, as Baez and Boyles do, "*which* public(s) does the university serve? If it
serves many publics, does it serve each equitably?"[53] With grants gaining
respectability (and—as we have seen—even becoming obligatory in some
cases) in higher education, critical educators must ask questions about *who*
grants serve. These are essential questions because it is always possible that
"universities will serve the private sector and overlook or ignore public or
altruistic goals."[54]

LACK OF IMPORTANCE GIVEN TO TEACHING

We have seen that most (70 percent) teaching is done by contingent labor and
that the "research stars" of the university often buy themselves out of most
teaching duties. This suggests that administration and faculty *alike* do not
think that teaching is important. How can our universities be social sites of
critical thought and inquiry if teaching is ignored and debased? If our very
own professors are not models of honest critical thinking in the classroom,
but rather spend the majority of their time getting their name in print for
careerist reasons; and if our own college leaders can only be expected to care
about education and perform their duties if they are granted paychecks hun-
dreds and thousands of percentage points over the average teacher—how can
we expect our students to *not* be narrowly careerist or self-absorbed in their
own lives? Don't we, professor and administrator alike, model the *very behavior* that we bemoan in our students? Oh those terrible students, grade-
grubbing and adding lines to their CVs—not caring at all about the intrinsic
good of learning literature, history, or physics! Not doing any honest critical
thinking about their place in the world! When is the last time one of us took a
class or studied a new field without instrumental reasons? Attended a guest
lecture that was not in our own discipline? The last time we spent hours
helping a student improve his or her work without the promise of our own
name being in print, or adding another line to our own CVs? Or openly posed
ethical questions about our own life choices?

Several additional reasons (in addition to the grants culture and the dependence upon cheap adjunct labor) have been offered as to how and why research became the holy grail of university work at the cost of devaluing teaching and service. (Some argue that teaching is not being devalued, that we are better teachers now precisely *because* research is so important. We will question that supposition in a moment.) How did we get to where we are? Some suggest that scholarship has become so important because it is easy to commodify, quantify, and count. We believe that we can state confidently that a professor who publishes five peer-reviewed journal articles is a better scholar than a professor who publishes one. (Though perhaps our confidence is unwarranted.) Thus the so-called "ratcheting up" of scholarship requirements for tenure and promotion: whereas thirty years ago at a medium-sized undergraduate college, one might be expected to publish two, one or no journal articles (but perhaps present a few articles at good conferences) in order to obtain tenure, now those same schools are requiring three, four or five single-authored journal articles. We think that we can claim that the professors now are "better" than the professors of thirty years ago. But what is the effect of these new scholarship criteria upon teaching? For professors as for everyone else, there are only twenty-four hours to the day. If one is expected to do more scholarship (in addition to more assessment, program review, budgeting, grant writing, and all of the other bureaucratic duties that modern professors are supposed to perform), then necessarily there is less time to read and grade student papers, to prepare and improve one's assignments and lectures, to read and view widely the things that might appeal to one's students, to support and attend campus events with colleagues and students, to welcome students to office hours or have other impromptu meetings with students and colleagues. Many faculty nowadays schedule a two-day week on campus; five days out of the week, they stay at home (presumably to do research) and two days per week they are on campus to teach classes and have office hours. Even office hours are becoming a quaint relic of the past as more and more professors claim that students can email them or message them with specific questions and that that is "just as good" as being bodily present for students on campus. Online courses can further instrumentalize the relations between professor and student as education becomes defined as the efficient transmission of data or skills from one person to another (more will be said about this in chapters 5 and 6). All around—from both faculty and administration—the expectation is that we should spend less time on teaching and student-related activities and more time on research.

Another reason given for why scholarship has become more important as opposed to teaching is that scholarship is "portable"—that is, if a professor is considering moving "up the ladder" to a better university ("better" usually defined circularly as those universities that have more scholars with more publications), one's record of scholarship will follow. On the other hand, how diligent or skilled one is at teaching and service is often a matter of "local knowledge." For instance, regarding service, it is very difficult to tell how dedicated of a committee member a person is—how much he or she contributes to the college community—just by reading his CV. He might have a long list of committee memberships but rarely attend meetings or contribute meaningfully to those groups. It should be no surprise that administration is assuming greater power in universities when many faculty members do not commit themselves to taking their service responsibilities seriously. It takes a lot of time and effort to be aware of all of the issues on campus—the staff, faculty and administrative hires or layoffs occurring; union negotiations with workers; possible changes to curricula or other education policy changes; the new buildings purchased; tuition rising, and so forth. A person committed to the college community will painstakingly build an awareness of these matters and will discuss them formally and informally with students and colleagues; insist on shared governance; and do the time-consuming work that shared governance requires. It doesn't seem entirely right to blame the administration for a power-grab on campus if professors are staying home five days a week, focusing energy primarily on research and grants and not on the wider college community. Merely complaining about the decisions of top administrators without the will or effort to change things does little good and often just creates a toxic environment on campus. We have to be aware of this behavior in our own ranks and call people on it when they engage in it. Many of us complain about the partisan bickering in our government without realizing that the same things are happening on our campuses. Commitment to the university community also requires honing and practicing the skills of honest and open debate. Just as we only become democratic when we practice democracy, shared governance also requires practice—and the more we practice, the better we become at it. Those practiced shared governors skilled in dialectic then become role models for others on the campus—newer faculty, but also staff, administration and our students. It is yet another way that we "teach" our students how to participate in a democracy, by listening and speaking with honesty and respect. Speaking truth to power is more easily engaged if one has witnessed others doing so. A critical university requires ongoing commitment to both teaching and service. It is part of the educational mission that serves our students that we build and maintain good organizational structures.

Everyone in higher education knows the whispered advice given to new tenure-track professors: Stay off of the labor-intensive committees, keep your head down, and don't waste too much of your time on teaching; spend every waking moment on scholarship. I wonder if our students know this?

Universities as critical sites of inquiry can only exist when professors themselves model critical life. This happens both in and outside of the classroom. In my classes, we often talk about current stories in the media as they relate to course readings, (e.g., the Trayvon Martin case along with Plato's ideas, the Detroit water crisis along with John Rawls's ideas, a current maintenance worker's strike on campus alongside Iris Marion Young's ideas). Last year on my campus, the Service Employees International Union (SEIU) workers were demonstrating for higher pay. A handful of professors encouraged our students to attend these rallies, listen to the workers' stories, and relate those stories to course content. It is this kind of analysis that will encourage our students to think critically about their own jobs and employers, the choices that they make as potential leaders and workers, and keep them mindful of the persons who surround them—in this case, the persons who may keep the lightbulbs replaced in their dorm rooms, keep their bathrooms clean, and replace the chalk in the classrooms. (In my *justice* course, the students listened to the workers' stories at the rallies, and one student wrote on her or his course evaluation "I never really thought about the human being who walked the halls at night checking to make sure each that each classroom has chalk in it. But now I know who that is and I know her name.") Baez and Boyles are correct: "The world can be transformed only when it is seen differently than before."[55] If we want to educate "whole persons" then we have to be whole persons connected to and committed to an analysis of broader society. Research, teaching, and service cannot be hermetically sealed inside our campuses or books.

Again, I do not think it is appropriate to blame the de-emphasis of teaching (and service) on administration, or at least not fully. I blame this shift on faculty themselves and on the systematic changes in higher education and the wider culture that are not entirely the fault of top administration.

We think we know good teaching when we see it. And we think we know bad teaching when we see it. But given that the vast majority of teaching might fall at neither end of the spectrum, how do we make sophisticated judgments about teaching? How do we reward the excellent teachers and inspire and assist the poor and mediocre teachers? Can we come up with an account of what good university teaching looks like? Can we write down what that is and measure people against that standard? This is a complex problem in higher education. Some may argue that judging teaching leads us into more neoliberalist territory—(i.e., more quantification and not less). That is a danger. But to do nothing is also a danger. To do nothing means we risk sticking with the system we have now where teaching is a pass/fail scale where we mostly just say regarding a person's teaching, "Well, it's *good enough*" as our eyes scan to their list of publications. As long as scholarship offers us varying levels of proficiency and teaching is considered pass/fail (with most everyone "passing"), people will achieve or be denied tenure based upon scholarship—and in fact, they will receive or not receive tenure-track jobs based upon scholarship. How can we expect our universities to be sites of critical thought and civil engagement if we do not hire on the basis of getting teachers who do that well?

Imagine that you are on the tenure review board of a university and you have candidates applying for tenure. In front of you are these candidates' course syllabi, sample assignments, examples of graded papers, grading distributions, peer observations, student evaluation scores, and student evaluation narrative comments with over 75 percent of students reporting. This is the minimal degree of evidence that you need in order to make sound judgments regarding a faculty member's teaching. Many schools place an excessive emphasis on a few quantitative measures. If there are universities that *only* use student evaluation quantitative scores (and I know that such schools exist) in order to judge teaching—clearly they are not doing a good job of evaluating or improving the teaching on their campus. For all of the complaining that faculty do regarding "ratemyprofessor.com"—it's unclear to me how it is all that different from the online student evaluations that most American universities use nowadays. We all know by now that many nonteaching variables effect those scores, grades given to students (thus grade inflation), gender/sex of the professor, age of professor, whether the student thinks the topic of the course is directly linked to their job prospects, and so forth. [56]

In his book, *Universities in the Marketplace: The Commercialization of Higher Education,* Derek Bok gives recommendations for how we might rank schools according to teaching. Therein he enumerates certain advantages of the competitive nature of the "marketplace" of higher education (he also mentions many of the drawbacks). [57] Bok writes, "*Competition* occurs when a number of actors vie with one another to reach a goal they cannot all achieve in equal measure," and "Although traditional universities are not organized to make a profit, they do compete vigorously with one another." [58] He points out that the *U.S. News and World Report* rankings of colleges and universities have become the standard way of gauging a university's success in the competitive field of higher education, although "the unreliability of these ratings is notorious, they continue to have an influence, since nothing else has been devised that provides such regular, seemingly exact measures of comparative academic quality." [59] Bok agrees that teaching has been lost in the shuffle. We have not devised a way of allowing universities to be compared in terms of what students will learn and how fulfilling that experience will be for them. At this moment in history, "rewards for excellent research far exceed those available for excellent teaching." [60] And, "[u]nder these conditions, competition does not necessarily cause good instruction to drive out bad." [61]

Under Bok's competition model, he believes that students should be able to seek which colleges would teach them the most and "soon, students would start to gravitate to the most effective schools" and faculty would want to be in those institutions where the best students were as well.[62] Bok asks whether this competitive model would be ideal for higher education—that is, if we could somehow measure and make widely available a ranking of schools where good teaching was favored above all other measures.

Bok makes an assumption about teaching and about the quality of one's education based on what I consider to be extreme elitism and ignorance. When discussing the possible growth of online education, some people have made the argument that what counts as "education" right now is not always the ideal picture of a close student-professor relationship with deep critical thought, engaging lectures and Socratic dialogue. And since that ideal is not happening anyway—so the argument goes—we might as well give students online education where they watch videos of professors speaking and take online multiple-choice exams. In other words, the claim goes, current education is not all that more engaging and life affirming than online classes. Bok writes, "It may not yet be possible to equal a truly well-taught Socratic discussion in a leading law school or the active give and take of a successful college seminar. Still, such on-campus experiences are not typical of the length and breadth of American higher education."[63] Then Bok quotes a student from a large state school:

> In my four years at . . . , I have had exactly four classes with under twenty-five students and a real professor in charge. All of the rest of my courses have been jumbo lectures with hundreds of students and a professor miles away, or classes with TAs . . . or [adjuncts –] people who come in off the streets to teach a course or two.[64]

But Bok makes a huge error in assuming that all non-Ivy-League or non-"leading" colleges have that kind of education. It is as if Bok believes that only places like Harvard have the Socratic classroom, close teacher-student relations, small classrooms, and engaging teachers. In fact, this is likely to be more true for the local community college or small private college that for the larger universities. The supposedly "leading" schools that Bok mentions are usually "leading" thanks to their rankings in the fame of their professors due to publishing. The "leading" schools are usually research-1 schools that are much more likely to have those 100-plus lecture halls taught by TAs. The real professors are too busy with grant applications and research. Bok assumes that leading schools have the best teachers: this is a dangerous assumption to make. We need to make a distinction between schools that lead in terms of research and schools that lead in terms of teaching. It is a mistake to think that a prolific scholar is also automatically a good teacher. It is a mistake to think that just because a college is prestigious (or has a large endowment) that most or all courses offered will be critically engaged, Socratic, and filled with professors who have a passion for interacting with their students. Typically, one gets offered a position at those elite schools because publishing has brought her or him renown—and again, there is no proof that being a star scholar means that one is an engaging teacher. Baez and Boyles take this assumption to task too: they claim that although this belief is widely held, there is no proof that high researchers make better teachers. [65]

I also want to ask a philosophical question about privileging scholarship over and above teaching and service in the modern university as this privileging relates to the notion of private property. Clear your mind of assumptions for the moment, and think of all of the ways in which a professor might be creative or innovative on a day-to-day basis. Then ask yourself: why does plagiarism (believed to be one of the worst sins that an academic could commit) generally apply only to scholarship? We glorify and protect a professor's work only as it relates to scholarship. When one thinks about all of the ways in which one uses one's talents, intelligence, problem solving, and creativity, it seems odd that only one type of labor is said to represent the individual. For instance, I have a colleague who chairs an important committee on our campus. Since becoming chair, he has revamped the way this committee works; it has become a more rigorous, more thoughtful, and more thorough committee that involves the voices of all people on that committee. Can we say with confidence that his work has done less for the world than another journal article would have? In other words, is it true that in every case a professor's research demonstrates his intelligence and creativity more than his service? Is the college or the world always improved by research more than by service? I have another colleague who was a long-time adjunct in the English department. He was known for being a fantastic teacher, the kind of teacher who inspires students long after they graduate. He doesn't get to put a big copyright TM mark after his teaching. "This is my teaching. I developed it. It's my creative genius." But this is something we do with scholarship. It is as if teaching and service are the more "communal" aspects of our work as professors, but our scholarship falls under the model of private property. Our research is "attached" to our names like private property; whereas, the innovation of our teaching and service are created and given to the world. (Granted a student has to pay money to get into the classroom— still, that tuition goes to the school, not the professor. And in the case of adjuncts—the majority of teachers—they see very little of that tuition.) Nor are faculty paid more or given more recognition if their teaching improves. Publishing another journal article gives faculty recognition in a way that creating a stimulating writing assignment for one's students does not. So, it is no surprise in this era, private-property inspired research is considered to be the thing that the "best" professors do the most of. More broadly, think about all of the work that goes on in the world, the acts of creativity and innovation that living beings perform every day. Which kinds of work get to be attached to which kinds of people? The ability to claim ones work as one's own is a privilege of the very few. And believing that universities ought to become sites of critical thought and inquiry may require that we rethink our priorities. We need to find ways of encouraging academics to put more of their critical thinking and creativity into their teaching.

DECREASE IN IMPORTANCE OF LIBERAL ARTS/HUMANITIES

President Obama has been weighing in on the benefits of a college education—those benefits that he believes are important for the nation as a whole. Unfortunately, he talks only about the *economic* benefits of higher education and not its civic and moral values—let alone how education might help human beings to live more fulfilling and meaningful lives. The assumption that President Obama and many others make is that wealth alone will, in every case, make for more fulfilling lives for citizens and a better society. If anyone should be talking about ethical citizenship, engagement, and the "pursuit of happiness" (whatever values we might decide 'happiness' embodies!) with regards to the virtues of education, one would hope that the president would be chief among them. Sadly, this is not the case. In his speech at the first White House Summit of Community Colleges in October, 2010, he discussed the importance of community colleges and applauded "partnerships" between community colleges and corporations such as McDonald's and the Gap, where community colleges provide training of practical skills to prepare students for the job market—specifically, McDonald's names the "skills" that it wants its workers to have (and of course, conversely, the skills and knowledge that it does *not* value), and the community colleges provide McDonald's with whatever it desires. [66] In this model, higher education is the handmaiden to the profits of the corporate world. Higher education may still nominally consist of not-for-profit organizations (in most cases, anyway, there are some for-profits entering the fold). Nonetheless, these not-for-profit organizations are often serving the whims and desires of private business interests and goals. One step removed, not-for-profit institutions are in fact serving the profit motive. People and their education have become mere tools to serve that aim. As Peter McLaren says, "The problem is that while schools should serve as the moral witnesses for the social world in which they are housed, they are today little more than functional sites for business-higher education partnerships." [67] Hardly anyone questions this logic or even draws attention to it. It has all come to seem so natural. And President Obama not only seems fine with this arrangement, he applauds it and suggests further development in this area.

In a 2013 speech on college affordability, President Obama says, "a higher education is the single best investment you can make in your future" and "the best ticket to upward mobility in America" that is "a necessity, an economic imperative."[68] Obama lists three things that the U.S. government is going to do regarding higher education and the first one is this: "come up with a new ratings system for colleges that will score colleges on . . . whether they have strong career potential."[69] We might ask a Socratic question to the President, one spelled out in *The Republic*, about the difference between *wisdom* and *skill*. Skill, according to Plato, is what the cobbler has in knowing how to make a great pair of shoes, or the baker has in baking a wonderful loaf of bread. Skill is certainly vital to the functioning *polis*. But wisdom is the investigation into how society should be structured such that the baker and the cobbler have a relationship of justice, how to live a good life as an individual and as a citizen, how to develop virtues and how to reason about what counts as virtuous, and how to have a well-balanced soul. This split between these two kinds of knowledge existed in ancient Roman culture, while slaves were readily encouraged to study professional skills; only the free citizens (*liberi*) were able to study the "liberal arts." Why? Well, slaves should not ask all of those pesky, big philosophical questions such as, 'What does it mean to be a person?' or 'What does it mean to have a just society?'—questions that threaten the status quo structure of any society at any time. President Obama, in emphasizing only career-skills acquisition in the college educations of lower-income citizens (by and large those who attend community colleges), is essentially saying the same thing said in Ancient Rome to the slaves: Keep your nose to the grindstone and make or sell products for the profit of others, but do not lift your head to the skies to ask any big questions about people, society, revolutions, historical movements, literature, art, justice, or morality. That is not wanted from you.

SUNY Albany cut and closed its departments in modern languages and theater in 2010. In an article published in the *New York Times*, Stanley Fish, responding to this closure, poses the question, "What will happen if we let the humanities die?" and adds, "if your criteria are productivity, efficiency and consumer satisfaction, it makes perfect sense to withdraw funds and material support from the humanities . . . and leave standing programs that have a more obvious relationship to a state's economic prosperity."[70] In short, what has happened in the past decade is rising support (even from the president) for teaching narrowly defined "McDonald's skills" and a dwindling of support for the humanities. In Martha Nussbaum's 2010 book, *Not for Profit: Why Democracy Needs the Humanities*, she argues that

> Radical changes are occurring in what democratic societies teach the young, and these changes have not been well thought through. Thirsty for national profit, nations, and their systems of education, are heedlessly discarding skills that are needed to keep democracies alive. If this trend continues, nations all over the world will soon be producing *generations of useful machines, rather than complete citizens* who can think for themselves, criticize tradition, and

understand the significance of another person's sufferings and achieve-
ments.[71]

She sums up: "The crisis is facing us, but we have not yet faced it."[72]
Nussbaum's book is important in thinking about what we want our universities to be because many have tried to claim over the years that the "pursuit
of economic growth will by itself" deliver other human goods such as health,
education, social equality, freedom, or economic equality.[73] And indeed,
what one hears both inside and outside the university is that a college's
number one priority is to get its graduates into high-paying jobs or into
graduate or professional schools that will give them high-paying jobs. Everything else is just "superfluous" or "icing on the cake" that could and should
be decided upon by individuals themselves (the neoliberal rhetoric of
"choice" is often used here)—after they have the kind of skills-training that
secures them high paying jobs. Nussbaum demonstrates that human goods
associated with fulfilling lives are very poorly correlated with economic
growth. I'll offer two of her examples: (1) China has had huge growth in
economics, but little growth in human liberty or political freedom; (2) South
Africa *while under apartheid* scored high marks in international development
indices and GNP. This leads to Nussbaum's thesis that "producing economic
growth does not mean producing democracy."[74] Democracies must be actively sustained by a certain type of citizen: curious, critical, reflective, active, rational, and capable of resisting authority and peer pressure. Furthermore (as I will later argue), training our students with *skills for jobs* without
critical education prepares them for lives of alienation. If we care about our
students as *whole persons*, we want them to have more than a high paycheck—we want to help prepare them to carry out good lives.

Also, if and when graduates do get fulfilling jobs, we want them to have
the reflective capacity and the courage to know when and how to question
their employers, when to strike or whistleblow on unethical behavior. We
don't, for instance, want workers to be versions of Hannah Arendt's Eichmann, a "perfect bureaucrat" who just does his job skillfully and efficiently
with little critical thought about what he is doing, why, and who and what his
work affects.[75] According to Arendt, Eichmann's biggest moral deficiency
consists in the fact that he was a dispassionate "recipient of orders"[76] used to
living his life obeying the authority and directives of his superiors,[77] and
blatantly unable to *think*, "to think from the standpoint of somebody else."[78]
A student who studies critical race theory, civil rights, labor history, animal
rights, feminism, and/or environmental movements is less likely to be passive, docile, or complacent when her job requires that she partake in some
version of oppressive behavior on others. Studying the lives of civil rights
heroes, for instance, can remind us of what critical, engaged human beings
are capable of.

In Herbert Marcuse's address on "Humanism and Humanity,"[79] he says that the traditional understanding of "humanism" is no longer up to the challenges of our time.

> Humanism was the intellectual movement that, since the close of the middle ages, saw to it that the study of classical antiquity would serve as one of the fundamental pre-conditions for the free development of the human personality and human individuality. The idea of education, the idea of culture, stood against everything barbaric, everything inhuman, unfree.[80]

But Marcuse makes us face a difficult truth: our current epoch might be more inhumane than previous epochs. The reason? Due to "given possibilities, technical possibilities, economic possibilities" it is conceivable for us to eliminate much of the injustice and oppression of the world.[81] We—in some way—choose not to. The degree of a culture's inhumanity "can be assessed in only one way: in comparison with the given possibilities of furnishing a human(e) existence for everyone."[82] Our living standards rise together with war, genocide and national aggressiveness—and the old concept of "humanity" and of being "humane" is not up to the task of fixing these problems. "[T]raditional humanism" is the "education of humanity to a sense of human inwardness and to a certain style of life" that was "in reality only accessible to the elite."[83] Humanism fled into the private world. It separated itself off from tackling the messiness and the difficulty of public problems. "One could be humane at home or on Sundays, but during the week one participated in the humiliation of humanity."[84] Marcuse warns us—like Arendt—against separating our private from our public lives, and saving our poetry, art, critical thinking, and ethics for the private realm (or the classroom?) only. Responsible education in the Humanities should never allow such a false separation between our public lives and private lives. Nor should it ever justify its existence in the academy as merely a mode of refined entertainment or acculturation, which in the end amounts to the humanities being a tool for enriching one's own private life in the "civilized" manner of the time. "One could be so proud of one's Goethe and one's Beethoven and at the same time construct concentration camps."[85]

There have been many defenses of the Humanities in the popular and academic press lately. As Alexander Beecroft writes in his blog post "Defenses of the Two Humanities: The Two Cultures," these defenses most commonly fall into one of two categories.[86] In the first category are those who defend the Humanities in the manner of Nussbaum: that the Humanities (and perhaps other fields too, but the Humanities are vital here) help us to pose questions about the purposes and values of democracy, equality, and life, and help us to perceive the world in many ways—through the visual arts, history, music, literature, through ethical reasoning, and rational argumenta-

tion. In a nutshell, a liberal arts education helps humans to live more reflective, curious, and fulfilling lives that also lead to a more democratic and just
society. In the second category are those who argue that the humanities
provide well the "skills" that companies want—reading, writing, critical
thinking—and that by cutting the humanities, we are cutting out the valuable
skills that would make our students more employable. There is considerable
data suggesting that a strong preparation in the Humanities is a good "investment" in one's career. For instance, it is often the case that students majoring
in philosophy, English or history outscore the students majoring in more
career-preparatory fields on standardized tests like the LSAT, MCAT, GRE,
and teacher's certification tests. [87] Furthermore, ten or twenty years after
graduation, the salaries of Humanities majors meet or exceed the salaries of
others. [88]

Ultimately, though, I believe that the second of these categories is sub-
sumable into the first category. The first defense of the Humanities is broader
because living life well requires that one have some basic necessities like
income, healthcare, and meaningful work. This is part of leading a good life.
But the first defense of humanities does not deny that. Whereas the second
defense of the Humanities implicitly suggests that all education is ultimately
instrumental—all education serves the purposes of capital. The second defense implies that if those in the Humanities are interested in saving themselves and their fields, then they must learn to speak the language of neoliberalist capitalism and the free market. In other words, the Humanities must
learn to "sell" themselves. (Explain how your English major will ultimately
help the McDonald's corporation in making higher profits.) To be clear, I
side with Nussbaum (and the first defense), which is not to say that I am
naive with regards to our students' needs to find employment. As I wrote
above, finding meaningful work is big part of a life well lived. Note that I
wrote "*meaningful* work" which is surely different than simply "finding
work" or "finding work that gives one a fat paycheck." Certainly we can all
agree that one can find a job and make a lot of money but still not live a
fulfilling and worthwhile life. Further, before a student even *chooses* a major
or a career path for herself (a privilege that most people in the world do not
have, by the way), she should do some broad and open-minded investigation
into which ways of thinking are most interesting to her, why, how that career
affects others and the environment. To ask these questions, one needs more
than specialized study in one's own field. So goes the traditional defense of a
robust liberal arts curriculum, a defense with which I vehemently agree and
not just because it makes our students more money but also because it inspires our students to respect and live more *life*.

In his book, *How to Find Fulfilling Work*, Roman Krznaric writes that in
choosing careers on the basis of security and pay, "we may be looking for
fulfilment in the wrong places—in *having* rather than in *being*, in accumulat-

ing possessions rather than in building nurturing, empathetic relations."[89] Krznaric counsels people who are unfulfilled in their jobs to get onto another track; he has seen surgeons, lawyers, IT specialists, and the like—people who spent years of higher education to reach their careers of security who then find out that they do not feel fulfilled at all by this career. Fewer than half of those in the Western world feel satisfied and fulfilled by their career: job satisfaction in the United States is at 45 percent and similarly, in Europe, 60 percent of the gainfully employed claim that they would choose a different career path if they could.[90] Krznaric writes, "It might be time to abandon the assumption that a career mainly driven by making money can buy us the purposeful, flourishing lives that we so dearly desire."[91] He also suggests that over-specialization is not making us happy and suggests that we be "wide achievers" rather than "high achievers": "For over a century, Western culture has been telling us that the best way to use our talents and be successful is to specialize and become an expert in a narrow field."[92] There is a danger in this specialization, for instance, "studies of surgeons reveal that those who only perform operations on tonsils or appendices soon begin to feel the tedium and become unhappy in their lucrative jobs."[93]

The broad liberal arts education does much to fight this tedium. A student who has had a rich taste of literature, art, history, languages, religious studies, and philosophy is likely to find interest in at least one or two of those fields. After a day of operating on tonsils all day, taking a class in art history, or being able to take a complex joy at the art gallery, may be just what one needs to live a more fulfilling and engaged life. "[O]ur culture of specialization conflicts with something most of us intuitively recognize," "we each have multiple selves" and a life of wide achieving (rather than high achieving) may "develop the many sides of who we are."[94] Studies in ethics in particular can help to prepare us for making the kinds of life choices that will lead to fulfilling lives. Relying on the work of Peter Singer, Krznaric writes that "our greatest hope for personal fulfilment is dedicating our lives—and if possible our *working* lives—to a 'transcendent cause' that is larger than ourselves, especially an ethical one such as animal rights, poverty alleviation or environmental justice."[95]

Though Krznaric lists admirable reasons for including a healthy amount of humanities courses in every college curriculum, it is in itself not enough because it may remain within a neoliberal ideology that stresses the importance of individual happiness. As Nussbaum points out, we should also defend the idea that higher education must serve the common good (it is—after all—the reason that it merits its nonprofit status). The task of university is not only to save our students from boring and alienated individual lives but also to improve the common lot. McLaren and da Silva write that many defenders of the humanities (mostly "bourgeois male academics" according to them) talk about university as a "highbrow paradise," and long for the simplified days where everyone agreed that the humanities had worth, the "Victorian salons and Tudor libraries . . . and *belles-lettristes* from ivy league schools" where Euro-American civilization keeps "the savage at bay."[96] Such conservative defenses of the humanities are not wanted here, for they repulse critical thought rather than encourage it. That is the "civilizing force" of the colonizers who believe that the humanities will teach the "others" how to be human just like them while simultaneously solidifying the view that white, bourgeois males deserve their rung at the top of the hierarchy. No, that is not our defense of the humanities here.

RISING COST AND COMMODIFICATION OF HIGHER EDUCATION

An undergraduate education that includes a healthy dose of the liberal arts and, in particular, the humanities, is the best way to prepare our students for fulfilling lives that include an awareness of and dedication to ethical concerns. To those who would say that not every person attends a college or university, I would say, "Yes, not now, but we should all be working toward a system where everyone can and at the same time that we are encouraging the intellectual wealth of our college campuses to be available to everyone in the community—whether they are college students, postal carriers, bus-drivers, and so forth." Making sure that our guest lectures, poetry readings, roundtable discussions, art shows and other campus special events are free and open to the public is a good start. And we should work towards the goal of ensuring that all tuition for accredited education is fully subsidized by the state. At the same time, those aspects of the college that do not have to do with educational mission should be separated out from the college. There is no justification for public funds earmarked for education to subsidize costly college marketing or extravagant college sports programs. Nor do I think that public funds should subsidize inequality. No more adjunct professors being paid $2,987 per three-credit course[97] while head basketball coaches in the NCAA tournament get paid nearly $1.8 million a year.[98] On the rising cost of higher education, Chomsky says,

> [I]t's hard to argue that there's any economic basis for it. Just take a look around the world: higher education is mostly free. In the countries with the highest education standards, let's say Finland, which is at the top all the time, higher education is free. And in a rich, successful capitalist country like Germany, it's free. In Mexico, a poor country, which has pretty decent education standards, considering the economic difficulties they face, it's free. In fact, look at the United States: if you go back to the 1940s and 50s, higher education was pretty close to free.[99]

The past ten years has seen many books and articles on the theme of the corporatization of higher education. One book receiving a lot of attention is the Bok book already referenced (*Universities in the Marketplace: The Commercialization of Higher Education*), which claims to take "the first comprehensive look at the growing commercialization of our academic institutions."[100] In the preface, after describing a set of dreams (nightmares) that he has about the commercialization of Harvard, he writes, "Observing these trends, I worry that commercialization may be changing the nature of academic institutions in ways we will come to regret. By trying so hard to acquire more money for their work, universities may compromise values that are essential to the continued confidence and loyalty of faculty, students, alumni, and even the general public."[101]

Bok defines "commercialization" in a narrow manner—far too narrow in my view. For him, commercialization in higher education applies to the attempt to sell what the university is offering, "efforts to sell the work of universities for a profit."[102] He pretends that this effort is separable from the general university culture. In a footnote, he says that "other" writers "speak expansively" of commercialization as

> (1) The influence of economic forces on universities (e.g., the growth of computer science majors and departments); (2) the influence of the surrounding corporate culture (e.g., the increased use on campuses of terms such as *CEO*, *bottom line* or *brand name*); (3) the influence of student career interests on the curriculum (e.g., more vocational courses); (4) efforts to economize university expenditures (hiring more adjunct teachers) or to use administrative methods adapted from business, or (5) attempts to quantify matters within the university that are not truly quantifiable, such as trying to express matters of value in monetary terms rather than qualitatively.[103]

In opposition to Bok's view, Michael Sandel and I are in agreement. In his book, *What Money Can't Buy: The Moral Limits of Markets*, Sandel talks about virtues that might be at stake when we place something within the market. Sandel is correct when he writes, "We live at a time when almost everything can be bought and sold."[104] And he goes on to give examples of how in our contemporary time, "almost everything is up for sale" including prison cell upgrades, Indian surrogate pregnancy, the right to immigrate to the United States, the right to shoot an endangered species, and admission of your child to a prestigious university.[105] He continues, "Over the past three decades, markets—and market values—have come to govern our lives as never before. We did not arrive at this condition through any deliberate choice. It is almost as if it came upon us."[106] The thesis of this work (like his earlier work *Justice*) is that we need to learn how to reason together (and discuss and argue together) about the best ways to live. As a modern Aristotelian, this is in keeping with his virtue ethics position: a society is always a collection of virtues and vices, and a good society is structured in such a way that we encourage the virtues and discourage the vices. In order to create that structure, we have to engage in debate about which virtues are worth holding and promoting. His argument against market-based thinking is that markets tend to do exactly what a bad society does: encourage the vices that humans might have. Therefore, "we need to rethink the role that markets should play in our society."[107] "Today, the logic of buying and selling no longer applies to material goods alone but increasingly governs the whole of life. It is time to ask whether we want to live this way."[108]

Some (like Bok, in fact) presume that "markets are inert," that they "do not affect the goods they exchange"[109] or that markets "don't pass judgment on the preferences they satisfy."[110] Like Sandel, I disagree. That is why we cannot limit our understanding of the commercialization of higher education to only those particular items that universities buy and sell. Market thinking has invaded and replaced other values in higher education. "Economists often assume that markets do not touch or taint the goods they regulate. But this is untrue. Markets leave their mark on social norms."[111] "[S]ome of the good things in life are corrupted or degraded if turned into commodities."[112] I agree with Sandel and disagree with Bok, and that it why in this book, when I refer to the commercialization of higher education, I include all of those items that Bok wants to leave out. Market thinking has clearly invaded higher education in many and far-reaching ways, and from my position, this manner of thinking is tainting and degrading the virtue of education. "Where markets erode nonmarket norms [we all] . . . have to decide whether this represents a loss worth caring about" and this "requires that we make a moral assessment."[113] This book is partly that: an invitation to us all to engage in ethical reflection upon higher education.

Nonetheless, Bok's narrowness aside, he does have some damning things to say about the effects of the modest commercialization that he does admit to. In his chapter on education and profit, he discusses for-profit, online education firms that partner with many of the "top tier" schools in the United States. The for-profit company U.Next uses the name of its partner institution and its star teachers as a "brand" in order to make higher profits. Most often, university administrators were setting up these partnerships with U.Next (or other for-profits) without the knowledge or consent of the wider university campus. Obviously, best practices in shared governance were not followed. He writes, "Negotiated behind closed doors without consultation with faculty or students, the contract drew a mixed response when it finally became public knowledge."[114] Bok also gives the example of the relationship between medical schools and the pharmaceutical industry, stating, "a full third of the total cost of continuing medical education is paid for by interested corporations."[115]

Hersh and Merrow's 2005 book, *Declining by Degrees: Higher Education at Risk,* has been at the heart of many discussions about the corporatization of higher education. The book has a companion PBS documentary. Tom Wolfe writes in the foreword, "You know, I come from a town, New York City, where families are rated according to whether or not their children get into Harvard. But I have never met a single parent—not one—who has ever shown the slightest curiosity about what happens to them once they get here."[116] I agree with Wolfe that in the nonacademic world there is much discussion about admissions and careers, steps 1 and 3 in a multistep process. We care about who gets into which prestigious college—in fact, in an odd circular motion, we rank colleges partly according to who they *don't* let in. Then we talk a lot about what jobs they get and how much those jobs pay. In other words, the nonacademic world (and increasingly, the academic world) talks about education as if it were merely a commodity (more on that in a later chapter). Indeed, Hersh and Merrrow wrote the book because they wanted to know what "actually happens between admission and graduation? How much 'deep learning' occurs? And when it does not, who should be held responsible?"[117] When we treat education as a commodity and an investment, critical education is lost. We end up treating human beings as nothing but economic tools—potential earners. If their education is commodified, they themselves are commodified and so are we. Faculty become toolmakers and shapers just as our students become tools. Tools do not need to think. In fact, it's preferable if they do not.

NOTES

1. "As of 2005, at least 70 percent of US faculty were teaching on contingent appointments," Marc Bosquet, "Management's *Kulturkampf,*" in *Academic Repression: Reflections from The Academic Industrial Complex,* ed. Anthony J. Nocella II, Steven Best, and Peter McLaren (Oakland: AK Press, 2010), 512; "About 70 percent of the instructional faculty at all colleges is off the tenure track, whether as part-timers or full-timers, a proportion that has crept higher over the past decade," Audrey Williams June, "Adjuncts Build Strength in Numbers," *The Chronicle of Higher Education,* November 5, 2012, http://chronicle.com/article/Adjuncts-Build-Strength-in/135520/; "The large and growing reliance on non-tenure-track faculty throughout higher education has resulted in such faculty members now accounting for approximately 70 percent of the faculty providing instruction at nonprofit institutions nationwide." Adrianna Kezar and Daniel Maxey, "The Changing Academic Workforce," *Trusteeship Magazine,* Association of Governing Boards of Universities and Colleges (AGB), May/June 2013, Number: 3, Volume: 21, http://agb.org/trusteeship/2013/5/changing-academic-workforce.
2. Cary Nelson, "The Three-Legged Stool: Shared Governance, Academic Freedom, and Tenure," in *Academic Repression: Reflections from The Academic Industrial Complex,* ed. Anthony J. Nocella II, Steven Best, and Peter McLaren (Oakland: AK Press, 2010), 474.
3. "There is a direct correlation between the development of a professionalized faculty, an increasing faculty role in institutional governance, and the unparalleled quality achievement by American higher education in the second half of the twentieth century." Larry G. Gerber, *The Rise and Decline of Faculty Governance: Professionalization and the Modern American University* (Baltimore: Johns Hopkins University Press, 2014), 6.

4. Henry Rosovsky, *The University: An Owner's Manual* (New York: W. W. Norton & Company, 1990), 165.

5. Rosovsky, *University: Owner's Manual*, 165.

6. "The court agreed that the faculty members are professional employees under § 2(12) of the [National Labor Relations Act (Act)], found that the Board had ignored 'the extensive control of Yeshiva's faculty' over academic and personnel decisions, as well as its 'crucial role . . . in determining other central policies of the institution,' and accordingly held that the faculty members are endowed with 'managerial status' sufficient to remove them from the Act's coverage." U.S. Supreme Court, *National Labor Relations Board v. Yeshiva University*, No. 78-857. Argued October 10, 1979, decided February 20, 1980. 444 U.S. 672, available at http://supreme.justia.com/cases/federal/us/444/672/. For a description of the case and the social forces and historical background surrounding it, please see Gerber, *Rise and Decline of Faculty Governance*, 130–39.

7. Gerber, *Rise and Decline of Faculty Governance*, 133.

8. Committee on Labor Relations, American Anthropological Association, *Resolution on Contingent & Part-time Academic Labor*, November 21, 2013, http://sunta.org/files/2010/12/Resolution-on-Contingent-Part-time-Academic-Labor.-.pdf.

9. Scott Jaschik, "Big Union Win," *Inside Higher Ed*, January 2, 2015, www.insidehighered.com/news/2015/01/02/nlrb-ruling-shifts-legal-ground-faculty-unions-private-colleges.

10. Jaschik, "Big Union Win."

11. Stanley Aronowitz, "Paulo Freire's Radical Democratic Humanism," in *Paulo Freire: A Critical Encounter*, ed. Peter McLaren and Peter Leonard (New York: Routledge, 2001), 21.

12. Aronowitz, "Paulo Freire's Radical Democratic Humanism," 21.

13. Benjamin Ginsberg, "Administrators Ate My Tuition," *Washington Monthly*, September/October 2011, www.washingtonmonthly.com/magazine/septemberoctober_2011/features/administrators_ate_my_tuition031641.php?page=all#.

14. Ginsberg, "Administrators Ate My Tuition."

15. Jay P. Greene, Brian Kisida, and Jonathan Mills, "Administrative Bloat at American Universities: The Real Reason for High Costs in Higher Education," *Goldwater Institute Policy Report*, No. 239, August 17, 2010, http://goldwaterinstitute.org/sites/default/files/Administrative%20Bloat.pdf.

See also: Noam Chomsky, "How America's Great University System Is Being Destroyed," *AlterNet*, February 28, 2014, www.alternet.org/corporate-accountability-and-workplace/chomsky-how-americas-great-university-system-getting?paging=off&current_page=1#bookmark; Benjamin Ginsberg, *The Fall of the Faculty: The Rise of the All-Administrative University and Why It Matters* (Oxford: Oxford University Press, 2011), and Douglas Belkin and Scott Thurm, "Deans List: Hiring Spree Fattens College Bureaucracy—And Tuition," The Wall Street Journal, December 28, 2012, http://online.wsj.com/news/articles/SB10001424127887323316804578161490716042814.

16. If we divide the number of administrators working full time in 2009 (222,282) by their number in 1989 (138,454), we can derive the percent increase for the period 1989–2009: approximately 60.5 percent. By comparison, over the same two periods (1999–2009 and 1989–2009) the number of full-time faculty rose by 37.2 and 61.9 percent respectively. These computations show that whereas both the number of full-time professional faculty and that of administrators tend to rise over time, the increase in the latter is much more rapid in the more recent time period. In fact, if we compare the data from this table to the respective number of institutions of higher education from Table 317.10, "Degree-granting postsecondary institutions, by control and level of institution: Selected years, 1949–50 through 2012–13," we can see that, on average, there were roughly 41 administrators per institution in 1989; for 2011, *ceteris paribus*, their number rose to 51 per school, a 25 percent jump.

From *The Digest of Education Statistics,* published by the National Center for Education Statistics, http://nces.ed.gov/programs/digest/d11/tables/dt11_257.asp and http://nces.ed.gov/programs/digest/d13/tables/dt13_317.10.asp.

17. Robert E. Martin and R. Carter Hill, "Baumol and Bowen Cost Effects in Research Universities," September 2012, www.wwu.edu/provost/communication/documents/Benchmark Report_FacultytoAdminRatio.pdf

18. Martin and Hill, "Baumol and Bowen Cost Effects in Research Universities."

19. Robert E. Martin, "College Costs Too Much Because Faculty Lack Power," *The Chronicle of Higher Education*, August 5, 2012, http://chronicle.com/article/College-Costs-Too-Much-Because/133357/.

20. Martin, "College Costs Too Much."

21. Jenny Rogers, "3 to 1: That's the Best Ratio of Tenure-Track Faculty to Administrators, a Study Concludes," *The Chronicle of Higher Education*, November 1, 2012, http://chronicle.com/article/Administrative-Bloat-How-Much/135500/.

22. See "Too Many Managers?," *SEIU Local 503*, April 7, 2011, www.seiu503.org/2011/04/too-many-managers/, and Neil A. G. McPhie et al, "As Supervisors Retire: An Opportunity to Reshape Organizations. A Report to the President and the Congress of the United States by the U.S. Merit Systems Protection Board," October 2009, www.mspb.gov/netsearch/viewdocs.aspx?docnumber=457394&version=458606.

23. "Wealthier institutions—such as research universities and private colleges—have been able to add instructional capacity at lower cost by hiring part-time faculty, while public nonresearch colleges have relied on these less-expensive instructors at the expense of full-time faculty. But at the same time, institutions have added new, nonfaculty professionals whose salary and benefits packages tend to be higher than those of part-time instructors (but less than full professors). Many of these new positions appear to be providing student services, but whether they represent justifiable expenses or unnecessary "bloat" is up for debate."

Delta Cost Project at American Institutes for Research, "Labor Intensive or Labor Expensive?," February 2014, http://www.deltacostproject.org/sites/default/files/products/DeltaCostAIR_Staffing_Brief_2_3_14.pdf.

24. Between June and July 2014, the college hired two new vice presidents: for enrollment management (www.canisius.edu/newsevents/davis-named-vice-president-for-enrollment-management-at-canisius-college), and for institutional advancement (www.canisius.edu/news-events/canisius-names-bill-collins-vp-for-institutional-advancement). Neither of these positions was a vice-presidential-level position ten years ago.

25. "As for other plans beyond the [retirement] buyout, it seems that, for now, the administration has run out of options and that layoffs [of tenure-track faculty] will be the next step. The hope that remains lies in the one year period between employees receiving termination notices and actually losing their job, during which natural shrinkage or alternative options can create additional openings." Jourdon LaBarber, "Retirement buyouts aim to minimize faculty layoffs," *The Griffin*, April 25, 2014, http://canisiusgriffin.com/?p=7430.

26. See Jay Tokasz, "Erie Community College creates new position despite revenue shortfalls," *The Buffalo News*, June 26, 2014, www.buffalonews.com/city-region/erie-community-college/erie-community-college-creates-new-position-despite-revenue-shortfalls-20140626.

27. Noam Chomsky, "How America's Great University System Is Being Destroyed," published online on *AlterNet*, February 28, 2014, www.alternet.org/corporate-accountability-and-workplace/chomsky-how-americas-great-university-system-getting?paging=off&current_page=1#bookmark.

28. Chomsky, "How America's Great University System Is Being Destroyed."

29. Chomsky, "How America's Great University System Is Being Destroyed."

30. Jonah Newman, "Highest-Paid Presidents Face Backlash, Study Finds," *The Chronicle of Higher Education*, December 15, 2013, http://chronicle.com/article/Highest-Paid-Presidents-Face/143599/.

31. Peter Jacobs, "The 10 Highest-Paid College Presidents," *Business Insider*, December 16, 2013, http://www.businessinsider.com/highest-paid-college-presidents-2013-12.

32. Jack Stripling and Jonah Newman, "4 Public-College Presidents Pass $1-Million Mark in Pay," *The Chronicle of Higher Education*, May 12, 2013, http://chronicle.com/article/4-Public-College-Chiefs-Pass/139189/. For a detailed list of the members of the "Million Dollar Club" of public and private university professors for 2010–12, see "Charts: When College Presidents Are Paid Like CEOs" by Jaeah Lee and Maggie Severns, *Mother Jones*, September

5, 2013, http://www.motherjones.com/politics/2013/09/charts-college-presidents-overpaid-pay. See also *The Chronicle*'s most recent report, "Executive Compensation at Public Colleges, 2013 Fiscal Year," May 16, 2014, http://chronicle.com/article/Executive-Compensation-at/ 146519/#id=table.

33. "Texas regents pick McRaven as chancellor finalist," *The Washington Post*, July 29, 2014, by Associated Press, http://www.washingtonpost.com/national/texas-regents-pick-mcraven-as-chancellor-finalist/2014/07/29/37d0de96-177b-11e4-88f7-96ed767bb747_story. html, and Charles Huckabee, "Admiral Is Named as Sole Finalist to Lead U. of Texas System, " *The Chronicle of Higher Education*, July 30, 2014, http://chronicle.com/blogs/ticker/admiral-is-named-as-sole-finalist-to-lead-u-of-texas-system/82909.

34. See, for instance, Section 489c in Book VI of Plato's *Republic*.

35. Robert Jensen, "Academic Freedom on the Rock(s): The Failures of Faculty in Tough Times," in *Academic Repression: Reflections from The Academic Industrial Complex*, ed. Anthony J. Nocella II, Steven Best, and Peter McLaren (Oakland: AK Press, 2010), 174.

36. Jensen, "Academic Freedom on the Rock(s)," 174–75.

37. Jensen, "Academic Freedom on the Rock(s)," 175.

38. Jensen, "Academic Freedom on the Rock(s)," 175.

39. Jensen, "Academic Freedom on the Rock(s)," 175.

40. Baez and Boyles, *Politics of Inquiry*, 211.

41. Baez and Boyles, *Politics of Inquiry*, 209.

42. Jensen, "Academic Freedom on the Rock(s)," 172.

43. Jensen, "Academic Freedom on the Rock(s)," 175–76.

44. Henry A. Giroux, *Neoliberalism's War on Higher Education* (Chicago: Haymarket Books, 2014), 146.

45. *The Future of Food*, directed by Deborah Koons Garcia (USA: Lily Films, 2004), DVD.

46. *The Future of Food*, 54:00–56:00.

47. Traditionally, the European Union (EU) has been decisively opposed to the imports and cultivation of genetically modified (GM) crops. However, "[o]n January 13th the European Parliament lifted the EU-wide ban, instead allowing national governments to impose their own restrictions. The plan has already been approved by governments, so the change should come into force this spring." ("Gently Modified," *The Economist*, January 17, 2015, www.economist.com/news/europe/21639578-eu-lifts-its-ban-gm-crops-gently-modified)

Some welcome this decision as an opportunity for individual member states to decide on their own restrictions without facing legal challenges from the EU as before, but others argue that "the new nation-oriented rules will allow more leeway for proponents of GM crops, such as Britain and the Iberian states, to go ahead." ("Monsanto-killer or 'Trojan Horse'? New law lets EU states ban GM crops," *RT News*, December 5, 2014, http://rt.com/news/211811-eu-gm-monsanto-trojan/).

Meanwhile, Chinese ports keep turning away U.S. imports claiming they have been tainted with GMO Syngenta corn, which "may cost U.S. growers as much as $6.3 billion in losses through August 2015." (Megan Durisin and Jeff Wilson, "U.S. Grain Losses Seen Up to $6.3 Billion on China Ban," *Bloomberg*, April 16, 2014, http://www.bloomberg.com/news/articles/2014-04-16/u-s-group-says-losses-may-be-6-3-billion-on-china-corn).

Several American states have also expressed interest in regulating GMO crops. The mandatory GMO labeling law the state of Vermont enacted in 2014—unprecedented in the United States, however, continues to face strong opposition from trade groups filing numerous lawsuits in an attempt to repeal it. (Niraj Chokshi, "Vermont just passed the nation's first GMO food labeling law. Now it prepares to get sued," *The Washington Post*, May 9, 2014, www.washingtonpost.com/blogs/govbeat/wp/2014/04/29/how-vermont-plans-to-defend-the-nations-first-gmo-law/.)

48. See for example: Vandana Shiva, *Ecology and the Politics of Survival: Conflicts over Natural Resources in India* (Thousand Oaks, CA: Sage Publications, 1991); *Biopiracy: The Plunder of Nature and Knowledge* (Cambridge, MA: South End Press, 1997); *Patents, Myths and Reality* (Penguin India, 2001); *Soil Not Oil* (South End Press, 2008).

49. *The Future of Food*, 01:07:00—01:14:00.

50. *The Future of Food*, 55:00—01:05:00.

51. *The Future of Food*, 55:00—01:05:00.

52. *The Future of Food*, 55:00—01:10:00.

53. Baez and Boyles, *Politics of Inquiry*, 201.

54. Baez and Boyles, *Politics of Inquiry*, 188.

55. Baez and Boyles, *Politics of Inquiry*, ix.

56. See, among others, Philip Stark, "Do Student Evaluations Measure Teaching Effectiveness?" on *The Berkeley Blog*, October 14, 2013, http://blogs.berkeley.edu/2013/10/14/do-student-evaluations-measure-teaching-effectiveness/; Rebecca Schuman, "Student Evaluations of Professors Aren't Just Biased and Absurd—They Don't Even Work," on *Slate*, April 24, 2014, www.slate.com/articles/life/education/2014/04/student_evaluations_of_college_profes sors_are_biased_and_worthless.html.

57. See Derek Bok, Ch. 9, "Preserving Educational Values" in *Universities in the Marketplace: The Commercialization of Higher Education* (Princeton, NJ: Princeton University Press, 2003), 159.

58. Bok, *Universities in the Marketplace*, 159.

59. Bok, *Universities in the Marketplace*, 159–60.

60. Bok, *Universities in the Marketplace*, 160.

61. Bok, *Universities in the Marketplace*, 161.

62. Bok, *Universities in the Marketplace*, 160–61.

63. Bok, *Universities in the Marketplace*, 88.

64. Bok, *Universities in the Marketplace*, 89.

65. See pages 167–171 in Baez and Boyles's book *The Politics of Inquiry*.

66. "Remarks by the President and Dr. Jill Biden at White House Summit on Community Colleges," The White House: Office of the Press Secretary, October 5, 2010, http://www.whitehouse.gov/the-press-office/2010/10/05/remarks-president-and-dr-jill-biden-white-house-summit-community-college.

67. Peter McLaren, "Educating for Social Justice and Liberation" in *Academic Repression: Reflections from The Academic Industrial Complex*, ed. Anthony J. Nocella II, Steven Best, and Peter McLaren (Oakland: AK Press, 2010), 502.

68. "Remarks by the President on College Affordability, Syracuse, NY" (The White House, Office of the Press Secretary), August 22, 103, www.whitehouse.gov/the-press-office/2013/08/23/remarks-president-college-affordability-syracuse-ny.

69. The second two goals of the Obama administration are (2) "to encourage more colleges to embrace innovation . . . creating partnerships between high schools and colleges so students can get a jump on their degree," (3) "make sure that if you've taken on debt to earn your degree that you can manage it and afford it." ("Remarks by the President on College Affordability, Syracuse, NY" (The White House: Office of the Press Secretary), August 22, 2013, www.whitehouse.gov/the-press-office/2013/08/23/remarks-president-college-affordability-syracuse-ny.

70. See Stanley Fish, "The Crisis of the Humanities Officially Arrives," *The New York Times*, October 11, 2010, http://opinionator.blogs.nytimes.com/2010/10/11/the-crisis-of-the-humanities-officially-arrives/?_php=true&_type=blogs&_r=0.

71. Martha Nussbaum, *Not For Profit: Why Democracy Needs the Humanities*, (Princeton, NJ: Princeton University Press, 2010), 2, my emphasis.

72. Nussbaum, *Not For Profit*, 2.

73. Nussbaum, *Not For Profit*, 15.

74. Nussbaum, *Not For Profit*, 15.

75. In 1961, *New Yorker* magazine sent political theorist Hannah Arendt to Jerusalem to report on Adolf Eichmann's trial. The articles that appeared as a result of this dispatch have subsequently been published under the title *Eichmann in Jerusalem: A Report on the Banality of Evil*. At the end of the last chapter of the book, "Judgment, Appeal, and Execution," Arendt introduces the phrase "the banality of evil," by means of which she seeks to explain the lack of resistance against the atrocities perpetrated by the Nazis during the Third Reich, and Eichmann's actions as part of the Nazi mass-murder machine in particular. She writes, for instance, that "[t]echnically and organizationally, Eichmann's position was not very high" (1963:65); that he was nothing more than a small cog "giving unquestioning obedience to the Führer's

orders" (1963:52), and that "[h]e did his *duty*, . . . he not only obeyed *orders*, he also obeyed the *law*." (1963:120) Arendt's analysis of Eichmann's career serves as an important warning about what the world can turn into if we don't exercise critical thinking and blindly follow orders.

76. Hannah Arendt, *Eichmann in Jerusalem: A Report on the Banality of Evil* (New York: The Viking Press, Inc., 1963), 24.

77. Arendt, *Eichmann in Jerusalem*, 28/88.

78. Arendt, *Eichmann in Jerusalem*, 44.

79. Found in the book *Crisis and Commonwealth: Marcuse, Marx, McLaren*, edited by Charles Reitz (Lexington Books, 2013).

80. Marcuse, "Humanism and Humanity" in *Crisis and Commonwealth*, 289.

81. Marcuse, "Humanism and Humanity" in *Crisis and Commonwealth*, 292.

82. Marcuse, "Humanism and Humanity" in *Crisis and Commonwealth*, 292.

83. Marcuse, "Humanism and Humanity" in *Crisis and Commonwealth*, 293.

84. Marcuse, "Humanism and Humanity" in *Crisis and Commonwealth*, 293.

85. Marcuse, "Humanism and Humanity" in *Crisis and Commonwealth*, 293.

86. Alex Beecroft, "Defenses of the Humanities: The Two Cultures," *A New Deal for the Humanities* (blog), January 25, 2014, http://newdealhumanities.com/2014/01/25/defenses-of-the-humanities-the-two-cultures/.

87. "A new study finds that the highest LSAT scores are achieved by students who major in physics/math, economics and philosophy/theology. Even more interesting is that the two majors that rank lowest in LSAT scores are the very two that provide training in law—prelaw and criminal justice." *Legal Blog Watch*, http://legalblogwatch.typepad.com/legal_blog_watch/2009/09/choice-of-college-major-sways-lsat-score.html.

Also see "Best Majors for GRE Scores in 2013: Philosophy Dominates," *Physics Central*, http://www.physicscentral.com/buzz/blog/index.cfm?postid=51120198413463888353, and reports of the humanities departments of Southern Utah University (http://suu.edu/hss/languages/philosophy/whystudy.html), Belmont University (http://www.belmont.edu/philosophy/general_information/), Drury University (http://humanities.drury.edu/?page_id=278), and Millsaps College (http://www.millsaps.edu/academics/philosophy_careers_for_philosophy_majors.php), among many others.

88. "Your parents might have worried when you chose Philosophy or International Relations as a major. But a year-long survey of 1.2 million people with only a bachelor's degree by PayScale Inc. shows that graduates in these subjects earned 103.5 percent and 97.8 percent more, respectively, about 10 years post-commencement." Cited from "Salary Increase By Major," *Wall Street Journal*, http://online.wsj.com/public/resources/documents/info-Degrees_that_Pay_you_Back-sort.html.

89. Roman Krznaric, *How to Find Fulfilling Work* (The school of Life 2012, Macmillan), 44.

90. Krznaric, *How to Find Fulfilling Work*, 8.

91. Krznaric, *How to Find Fulfilling Work*, 44.

92. Krznaric, *How to Find Fulfilling Work*, 59.

93. Krznaric, *How to Find Fulfilling Work*, 59.

94. Krznaric, *How to Find Fulfilling Work*, 59–60.

95. Krznaric, *How to Find Fulfilling Work*, 50.

96. Colin Lankshear, "Functional Literacy from a Freirean Point of View" in *Paulo Freire: A Critical Encounter*, ed. Peter McLaren and Peter Leonard (New York: Routledge, 2001), 50.

97. Data from *The Adjunct Project*, http://adjunct.chronicle.com/, and Audrey Williams June and Jonah Newman, "Adjunct Project Reveals Wide Range in Pay," *The Chronicle of Higher Education*, January 4, 2013, http://chronicle.com/article/Adjunct_Pay_Conditions/136439/.

98. Josh Peter and Steve Berkowitz, "Special report: Coaches hit jackpot in NCAA system," *USA TODAY Sports*, April 2, 2014, www.usatoday.com/story/sports/ncaab/2014/04/02/ncaa-tournament-basketball-coaches-compensation-obannon-case/7208877/. In fact, the top five conferences in major college sports may have just become more powerful, as the NCAA Division I board of directors voted 16–2 to allow them even more autonomy to make decisions about insurance benefits for players, staff sizes, recruiting rules, and mandatory hours spent on

individual sports. For more details on what that decision entails, see Brian Bennett, "NCAA board votes to allow autonomy," *ESPN College Sports*, August 8, 2014, http://espn.go.com/college-sports/story/_/id/11321551/ncaa-board-votes-allow-autonomy-five-power-conferences.

99. Chomsky, "How America's Great University System Is Being Destroyed."

100. Derek Bok, *Universities in the Marketplace: The Commercialization of Higher Education,* (Princeton and Oxford: Princeton University Press, 2003), book jacket.

101. Bok, *Universities in the Marketplace*, x.

102. Bok, *Universities in the Marketplace*, 3.

103. Bok, *Universities in the Marketplace*, 3.

104. Michael Sandel, *What Money Can't Buy: The Moral Limits of Markets* (New York: Farrar, Straus and Giroux, 2012), 5.

105. See Sandel, *What Money Can't Buy*, 3–4.

106. Sandel, *What Money Can't Buy*, 5.

107. Sandel, *What Money Can't Buy*, 7.

108. Sandel, *What Money Can't Buy*, 6.

109. Sandel, *What Money Can't Buy*, 9.

110. Sandel, *What Money Can't Buy*, 14.

111. Sandel, *What Money Can't Buy*, 64.

112. Sandel, *What Money Can't Buy*, 10.

113. Sandel, *What Money Can't Buy*, 90.

114. Bok, *Universities in the Marketplace*, 80.

115. Bok, *Universities in the Marketplace*, 86.

116. Tom Wolfe, *Declining by Degrees: Higher Education at Risk,* ed. Richard H. Hersh and John Merrow (New York: Palgrave MacMillan, 2006), x.

117. Richard H. Hersch and John Merrow, *Declining by Degrees*, 2.

Chapter Two

Radical Teaching

We have surveyed the situation on-the-ground in contemporary higher education. The center of this book will seem a little less practical and a little more idealistic. But I reject the notion that the idealistic is not practical. We cannot build good systems without thinking carefully and idealistically about what good systems look like and how and why they function. I want us to think about what we desire our universities to become. Put aside for the moment your doubts and skepticism—ultimately, they will keep us trapped where we are. Try to imagine universities as integral organizations to a just society. What would those universities teach? Who would they teach? How would they function? I am going to argue that the university's main goal in society is to be *a place to think*. That sounds innocuous and vague. It isn't— we'll get more specific and define this power as we go along. The path that I am asking you to walk with me moves through some complex philosopher's ideas—ideas that I believe will help us to become clear on why and how universities should exist.

This chapter locates itself within the bold proclamation of Herbert Marcuse in his book, *The Aesthetic Dimension: Toward a Critique of Marxist Aesthetics*. In this, his final book, Marcuse criticizes Marxism (and most Marxists) for taking too narrow of an approach to revolution and thus not seeing the ways in which civilization moves or progresses—thus not being able to grasp the various ways of revolution that would make sense and promote liberation and the just community. Marxists, he claims, have largely ignored the individual and the emotional life of the individual, thus ignoring a large possible site of revolution. This is perhaps their greatest fault and blind spot in desiring revolution. When we seek a just community, we must at the same time discuss the individual and her oppressors. From this foundation based on Marcuse's ideas, I move to the argument of Julia Kristeva in

"Psychoanalysis and Freedom," from her book *Intimate Revolt: The Powers and Limits of Psychoanalysis*. Therein, she describes the process of analysis as an act of liberating the individual. But, as we will see, this liberation is not freedom *from* the community, but freedom to engage. I follow the path of her argument all the while dissecting the process—not of analysis—but of radical teaching. This chapter overall defends two positions, the first inspired by Kristeva and the second by Marcuse: (1) that radical teaching is an act of freeing the individual and (2) that just communities can be sought by liberated individuals, who are in a continual state of revolution/revolutionizing.

MARCUSE

Let's look at the last work that Marcuse wrote, *The Aesthetic Dimension: Toward a Critique of Marxist Aesthetics* (1978). We'll then take a brief look at Marcuse's work on Freud (*The Eros of Civilization*) that will lead us to Kristeva's comments on revolution and psychoanalysis. *The Aesthetic Dimension* is a fascinating (and to my mind, damning and accurate) description of the kinds of liberation we now need and how they might arise. His main point, with which I heartily agree, is that revolution has been framed only in terms of large-scale social movements—typically in or against government. The French Revolution is held up as the epitome of this kind of revolution: an entire people rise up together to fight a system which takes no account of their interests. I argue, alongside Marcuse, that this is a far too narrow definition of revolution. In fact, it is not the kind of revolution which is most likely, or even likely, to bring about the kinds of changes that we need in our current society.

Marcuse writes,

> The subjectivity of individuals, their own consciousness and unconscious tends to be dissolved into class consciousness. Thereby, a major prerequisite of revolution is minimized, namely, the fact that the need for radical change must be rooted in the subjectivity of individuals themselves, in their intelligence and their passions, their drives and their goals. [1]

In Marxism, he writes, "Subjectivity became an atom of objectivity;" [2] whereas what Marcuse hopes for is the "rebirth of the rebellious subjectivity." [3] Art is invaluable in this rebirth. The work of art "re-presents reality while accusing it," [4] and "stands under the law of the given, while transgressing this law," [5] and has the "power to break the monopoly of established reality." [6]

Charles Reitz, in his book *Art, Alienation and the Humanities*, claims that in *The Aesthetic Dimension*, "there is a 'turn' in Marcuse's theorizing, almost a reversal," away from the "militant activist positions" of his earlier works "to an explicit reassertion of certain of the most contemplative values and assumptions of classical European aesthetics."[7] I agree with Reitz that there is a marked shift in Marcuse's work by the time of his writing *The Aesthetic Dimension*, but I disagree that Marcuse loses or departs from any of his "militant activist positions." Those activist positions have now found hope for revolution from within the aesthetic experience, as an additional and crucial site of revolution. This is the revolution of individuals, their "passions, drives and goals" as quoted above. Revolution cannot take place at the level of class alone, Marcuse realizes by the time he writes his final work. He explains,

> Art can preserve its truth, it can make conscious the necessity of change, only when it obeys its own law against that of reality. . . . Art cannot change the world, but it can contribute to changing the consciousness and drives of the men and women who could change the world.[8]

Marxist aesthetics, unfortunately, devalues "the entire realm of subjectivity."[9] This is "reductionistic" and "brackets the particular content of individual consciousness and, with it, the subjective potential for revolution."[10]

I am not clear whether Marcuse believes that *only* art can provoke this subjective revolutionary potential. Because it is clear that I want to take Marcuse's ideas in a slightly different direction (toward teaching and ultimately to the structure of higher education), I will own up to the fact that in many places in the text, Marcuse does seem to be arguing that *only art* can bring the kind of shift he seeks. In this sense, there are several places in the text where Marcuse's argument is working against mine.

Such examples include the following few passages:

1. The thesis of the book is that "the radical qualities of art, that is to say, its indictment of the established reality and its invocation of the beautiful image (*schöner Schein*) of liberation are grounded precisely in the dimensions where art *transcends* its social determination and emancipates itself."[11]

2. "And in the intellectual culture of our society, it is the aesthetic form which, by virtue of its otherness, can stand up against this integration."[12]

3. "The revolution is for the sake of life, not death. Here is the perhaps most profound kinship between art and revolution."[13]

4. And most clearly, "Art breaks open a dimension inaccessible to other experience, a dimension in which human beings, nature, and things no longer stand under the law of the established reality principle."[14] Or more simply, "the truth of art lies in its power to break the monopoly of established reality."[15]

On the other hand, I want to keep Marcuse's over-all critique that Marxist theory has been blind to the plural modes of revolution. I would say not just Marxist notions, but popular notions of what a revolution is and how it operates have been constituted by this narrowness. I end this section by listing some of Marcuse's passages that support my goal. They include the following passages:

1. Marcuse claims we need to shift "the locus of the individual's realization from the domain of the performance principle and the profit motive to that of the inner resources of the human being: passion, imagination, conscience."[16]
2. But this is not mere inwardness and withdrawal from society; this shift in conscience must strive to "break out" into "the material and intellectual culture."[17]
3. Most important, throughout the text Marcuse emphasizes our paying attention to the drives, desires and emotions of individuals (which the earlier passages I've cited attest to).

HART ON THE PHENOMENOLOGICAL REDUCTION

In widening what we mean by revolution, alongside Marcuse, I reap ideas from James G. Hart's theory of the university and the humanities as spelled out in his astute article, "The Essential Look (*eidos*) of the Humanities." Therein, Hart masterfully applies the Husserlian notion of the *epoché* to modes of learning in the university. He offers a harsh criticism of the modern American university, which is today hardly more than "a contingent assortment of unrelated and capricious departments housed in a kind of department store for consumers looking for job training."[18] He laments that the "departments in the store" of the university are seen as successful to the degree that they "advance the growth interests of the corporations, the degree to which the university is able to serve the nationalist or imperialist impulses of the state," and observes that, under this system, "the nature of the university becomes increasingly occluded by and subordinated to capitalist economics and nation-statism."[19] Further, "money transfer, capital and investment possibilities" are the center of the university's concerns and what "seems to carry most weight" are "student recruitment, administration politics, the athletic department, the university offices for economic development, [ROTC], the School of Business, the amount of corporate and government grants given to the faculty, the size of the super computer, the number of superstars residing in and orbiting around the particular university" and so forth.[20] In the university defined thusly, "the humanities become the whimsical wispy decoration for the real work of the university."[21] So, what is to be done, what is the way out? Where is the revolutionary potential in our universities (again, other than in the obvious places like encouraging students to protest and the like)?

Hart argues that within the broad spectrum of programs and departments within the university, *the humanities can serve as the phenomenological reduction*. Hart writes, "Much of the modern university, and surely the ancient one too, functions in what phenomenology calls the 'natural attitude.' This attitude is how we are for the most part in the world."[22] The phenomenological reduction is the bracketing of the natural attitude that we usually take with regards to the world around us—the things we assume, the attitudes and stances that we take for granted. Whereas the *epoché* [bracketing] tries to bring us to a neutral stance, neither affirming nor denying the 'facts' of the world and ourselves. It is in this way that consciousness and the world can be explored with less bias or predisposition. It doesn't ask about the objects of perception, but steps back to ask, what is perception—how do we arrive at it? Hart admits that if the biologist is "finding out the DNA structure of a species of soy bean," then for her it might be an "unnatural" and "distracting intrusion" to reflect upon the act of perception itself.[23] So, Hart is not suggesting that the reduction *replace* all other forms of research. The problem is that "to the extent that the scientistic or naturalistic attitude gains a hegemony in all facets of our life," at that point "the natural sciences appear as the only true forms of knowing and all the other disciplines must take their bearings from these."[24] "The natural attitude is normative here as well in almost all of our life," whereas "[r]eflection on the *bringing to light* rather than on *what* is brought to light" is the task of those of us in the humanities.[25]

Hart's critique of the modern university helps me to spell out what I'd like to do with late Marcuse: use Marcuse's ideas on the revolution of the individual (through art), and apply them to the manner in which universities can and should teach as sites of radical critique, in the original meaning of that term, turning to the root of how, what and why we study at all. Now I turn to Kristeva, who helps me to further explain revolution through the freedom of the individual as a rebirth.

KRISTEVA

I chose to use a text of Kristeva's on psychoanalysis to talk about freedom and teaching and did so for (at least) two reasons: (1) there is plenty of literature on radical teaching from the likes of Paulo Freire and his many followers, and (2) Kristeva, within the first line of the article which I will rely heavily upon, admits that "Freedom is not a psychoanalytic concept."[26] Yet, despite her beginnings, by the end of the article, freedom is where she has arrived.

According to Kristeva, freedom is the ultimate goal in psychoanalysis, although of course, at the same time, hardly any philosopher in the past fifty years (at least within the continental tradition) believes of the complete freedom and autonomy of the subject. Postmodern theory has itself (in league with psychoanalysis) been charged with being utterly apolitical and relativistic (a charge mostly seen in the United States). Recall, for instance, the vitriolic attacks on Jacques Derrida—in place of obituaries—that ran in papers like *The New York Times* the day after his death. In a more academic vein, Fredric Jameson accuses postmodernism of being about superficiality, commodification, ahistoricism, and "essential triviality"—although to be fair, he makes these charges in order to raise expectations of those in postmodern times.[27] He writes that within the postmodern milieu, it will be nearly impossible "for political groups . . . to intervene in history and to modify its otherwise passive momentum," since this postmodern mode of being transforms the past "into visual mirages, stereotypes, or texts, effectively abolish[ing] any practical sense of the future and of the collective project."[28] These issues have been carefully elucidated by Douglas Kellner and Steven Best in their works, *Postmodern Theory: Critical Interrogations* (1991) and *The Postmodern Turn* (1997), or succinctly in their "Postmodern Politics and the Battle for the Future."[29] "As with postmodern theory, there is no one 'postmodern politics,' but rather a conflicting set of positions that emerges from the ambiguities of social change and multiple postmodern theoretical perspectives."[30] Postmodern theory has been charged with being apolitical. There is evidence for it: for instance, in the work of Foucault, a certain reading could lead one to the impression that the subject has no power, no possibility for an authentic or self-directed subjectivity outside of the power structures that shape and define us. There is also evidence against it: for instance in Derrida's work readers find a profound and endless ethical and political duty placed on the subject. As John Caputo writes in his obituary of Derrida,

> Deconstruction, it turns out, is not nihilism; it just has high standards! Deconstruction is satisfied with nothing because it is waiting for the Messiah, which Derrida translated into the philosophical figure of the "to come" (*à venir*), the very figure of the future (*l'avenir*), of hope and expectation Deconstruction's meditation on the contingency of our beliefs and practices—on democracy, for example—is made in the name of a promise that is astir in them, for example, of a democracy "to come" for which every existing democracy is but a faint predecessor state.[31]

I stand with the latter position—those like Derrida and his readers Caputo and Butler (amongst many others) who—although admitting that there is no central "I," and no "I" outside of the structures, systems and symbolic order that form us and our desires—believe nonetheless that there is room for the profound and deep responsibility (and the possible freedom) of the individual. I believe that freedom is not a given, but a task or a *goal*. There is no "core" of freedom underneath the layers of our oppressions (as if it were there all along waiting to be unburied). Instead, freedom is something that must be *built*. Autonomy does not exist first, and is then stripped away. Autonomy—never total—is a goal.

Kristeva's article follows the trajectory of freedom in psychoanalytic thought. She begins with Freud who assigns freedom "the meaning of an instinctual impulse, shackled by the human need to live in a community."[32] For Freud, freedom stands up against and is antagonistic to, civilization. To quote *Civilization and Its Discontents*, "The liberty of the individual is no gift of civilization" and "The urge for freedom, therefore, is directed against particular forms and demands of civilization or against civilization altogether."[33] Kristeva writes that for Freud, "[m]oral consciousness and its organ, the superego, thus impose from mankind's beginnings a renouncement of the instinctual freedom."[34] Yet, at the same time, Freud warns us against a kind of nostalgia: "It seems certain that we do not feel comfortable in our present-day civilization . . . it is very difficult to form an opinion whether and in what degree men of an earlier age felt happier."[35] In fact, Freud writes, "When we start considering this possibility, we come upon a contention which is so astounding what we must dwell upon it. This contention holds that what we call our civilization is largely responsible for our misery, and that we should be much happier if we gave it up and returned to primitive conditions."[36] Freud's understanding of freedom is thus a naturalist, "I can" understanding of caprice and drive without restriction—yet that does not imply that freedom is a higher or better state than man in civilized life. This drive becomes desire through understanding that a mature human can only think of desires and freedom through communally shared language that "checks impulse and command."[37]

Kristeva follows the path from Freud to Lacan. Yet, to my mind, Kristeva's reading of Lacan is more innovative than she gives herself credit for. She claims that Lacan maintains "subjective interiority" radicalized "to the extreme."[38] Through the process of analysis, the subject is now authorized to "discover his desire and to explore his own limits."[39] Though, of course, this authorization is always already structured by the language, forces, expectations, norms, hierarchies—in short, by the symbolic order in which she must find her place. I always read Lacan as leaving very little wiggle room for the subject to do any of her own discovery of desire that "own" being a construction anyway since the subject is always already in the grips of the non-subjective. In Freud's terminology, the subject can never and will never escape civilization and thus can never really be "free" in the pure "naturalist" sense that Kristeva first describes. It is the new freedom, freedom as desire and not drive, that Kristeva explores and finds fertile.

That psychoanalysis is "antinormativist" is clear. Both Kristeva and Paul Ricoeur (in his book on Freud)[40] write about this: that in behaviorist therapy (and other forms of "ego psychology" prevalent especially in the United States), the overall goal of engaging in therapy is to get the patient in-line with the "norm" of society. Of course, this brings several problems for feminists and those who fight for justice. Why "normatize" people to an unjust world? A therapist is then a collaborationist with injustice, by "healing/aligning" a patient to the systems and ideals of an unjust society. (One need only think of being a woman in so-called "marriage therapy" in the mid-twentieth-century to imagine this kind of hell!) I am in complete agreement with Kristeva when she writes that psychoanalysis is "not only antinormativist" but "in implicit polemic with ego psychology," which points to the "discomfort" that psychoanalysis always encounters and "will always encounter" in "the moralizing universe of technology and adaptation."[41]

I argue that a parallel can be drawn between behaviorist therapy and the kind of "normativist" teaching that would be a collusion with what Hart calls the "natural attitude" of the world and university—an education that replicates the corporate model of beliefs, similar to what Freire called the "banking" concept of education (see chapter 2 of his *Pedagogy of the Oppressed*). This is education as an accumulation of facts that *matter to* and *prepare us for* the present state of (unquestioned) affairs and values. To keep with Kristeva's language, this is what we might call a "normativist" education, where what Freire (and I) are pushing for is an "antinormativist" education, just as psychoanalysis is an antinormative therapy. Let me sketch a kind of *momentary polemic* for the purposes of just the kind of *dichotomy* that Kristeva suggests:

Behaviorist therapy	< ——————— >	Psychoanalysis
Current state of the university	< ——————— >	Humanities
Normative	< ——————— >	Radical

CONCLUSION

If we return to Hart, we recall that he claimed that most of what was going on in the contemporary university was "normative"—that the natural attitude is normative, and that the humanities have the most radical potential due to the *epoché* that they can provoke. According to Kristeva, Lacan's ideal in therapy is neither to bend the patient to the society that surrounds him, nor to let the subject have free rein on his desires. Here is a passage where Kristeva describes the kind of freedom that is possible in Lacanian psychoanalysis:

For if the analyst's benevolent neutrality allows the patient not to yield to his desire, it is not less true that we greet this freedom with a certain number of ideals. . . . His listening and interpretation welcome these desires based on a moral choice that constitutes an ethic; it is not instructive, but it is not without communal objectives . . . Lacan himself evokes a few of his ideals: to make the patient capable of love, to favor authenticity against "as if" personalities or "false selves," to reinforce independence.[42]

If psychoanalysis works, it puts the subject into a constant state of rebirth. This is a rebirth of the subject not internally so that one could be free *from* others, but freedom to internalize the outside and to engage *with* others. Here Kristeva's originality shines. She describes a mature subject free from acting defensively toward the outside world, toward the community. The perpetual rebirth that she describes is rebirth to openness. Her hopes for psychoanalysis are high. She writes, "Let us say without false modesty: no modern human experience aside from psychoanalysis offers man the chance to restart his psychical life and thus, quite simply, life itself, opening up choices that guarantee the *plurality of an individual's capacity for connection.*"[43] And she continues, "This version of freedom is perhaps the most precious and most serious gift that psychoanalysis has given mankind."[44] For Kristeva, psychoanalysis is one part of civilization that—contra Freud, rather than decreasing an individual's freedom—increases her freedom by fostering her ability to make connections and links. It is by understanding ourselves, our history, and *how* we have othered others in our lives, that from that understanding we are able, from this understanding, to "rebirth" ourselves into new relations, new others, new eyes.

This rebirthing of the self is precisely what Kristeva denotes when she reminds us that the original meaning of revolution—revolt—is indeed to cause a re-birthing, a new start, a turning around. In another work, *The Sense and Non-Sense of Revolt*, she turns our attention to the etymology through the Latin words *volvere* and *volte* and links them to the derivative terms *curve, curvature,* and *turn/return,* but also movement in time such as *turning back* or *wrapping* amongst others.[45] This revolting of the subject allows him to "attenuate his sufferings, to relocate his desires, and to restart his creativity—indefinitely."[46] One of the final points that she makes in her essay is that "[t]he aptitude for this revolt leads the analyzed person to re-create links, suggesting that the analytical experience is at the source of a serious humanism."[47] I suggested earlier that freedom is not a given, but a *goal*; that autonomy is not at our core, but is to be *built*. Alongside Kristeva, I believe that this autonomy is never built apart from others and in opposition to them, but in concert with them and with their assistance. Others help me (and I can choose to help them), remove my (and their) blocks toward openness per se.

M. Jacqui Alexander, in her book *Pedagogies of Crossing*, compares the economy and the academy. One manner of comparison is that "universities provide workers for the economy."[48] And she writes that the "ideological attack" against multiculturalism and feminism makes a statement about "the kind of worker that the transnational empire requires—a worker who fits into an already assigned place within the productive process, without a critical examination of how she got there and who is there with her."[49] Bad teaching and bad therapy have a similar—though usually unspoken—goal, and Alexander describes it well: a human who "fits into an already assigned place," be that a worker on the assembly line, a student in medical school, a "good wife," or "a breadwinner for the family." What I am suggesting has similarities to Heidegger's sense of *das Nicht-zuhause-sein*—that which constantly reminds us that we are not at home, that authenticity requires that we always question our home, our "assignment," our place in the world.[50] Radical education undoes the assignment of place. It unassigns and rebirths, not just once, but sets up that revolting to occur throughout one's life.

NOTES

1. Marcuse, Herbert, *The Aesthetic Dimension: Toward a Critique of Marxist Aesthetics*, (Boston: Beacon Press, 1978), 3–4.

2. Marcuse, *Aesthetic Dimension*, 4.

3. Marcuse, *Aesthetic Dimension*, 7.

4. Marcuse, *Aesthetic Dimension*, 8.

5. Marcuse, *Aesthetic Dimension*, 11.

6. Marcuse, *Aesthetic Dimension*, 9.

7. Charles Reitz, *Art, Alienation, and the Humanities: A Critical Engagement with Herbert Marcuse* (Albany: State University of New York Press, 2000), 195.

8. Marcuse, Herbert, *Aesthetic Dimension*, 32.

9. Marcuse, *Aesthetic Dimension*, 3.

10. Marcuse, *Aesthetic Dimension*, 4.

11. Marcuse, *Aesthetic Dimension*, 6.

12. Marcuse, *Aesthetic Dimension*, 50.

13. Marcuse, *Aesthetic Dimension*, 56.

14. Marcuse, *Aesthetic Dimension*, 72.

15. Marcuse, *Aesthetic Dimension*, 9.

16. Marcuse, *Aesthetic Dimension*, 5.

17. Marcuse, *Aesthetic Dimension*, 5.

18. James G. Hart, "The Essential Look (*eidos*) of the Humanities: A Husserlian Phenomenology of the University," *Tijdschrift voor Filosofie*, 70 (2008), 110.

19. Hart, "Essential Look," 111.

20. Hart, "Essential Look," 110–11.

21. Hart, "Essential Look," 111.

22. Hart, "Essential Look," 113.

23. Hart, "Essential Look," 114.

24. Hart, "Essential Look," 115.

25. Hart, "Essential Look," 114.

26. Julia Kristeva, *Intimate Revolt: The Powers and Limits of Psychoanalysis, Vol. 2*, trans. Jeanine Herman (New York: Columbia University Press, 2002), 225.

27. Fredric, Jameson, *Postmodernism, or, the Cultural Logic of Late Capitalism* (Durham, NC: Duke University Press, 1991), 46.

28. Jameson, *Postmodernism*, 46.

29. Steven Best and Douglas Kellner, "Postmodern politics and the battle for the future," *Illuminations*, 2002, www.uta.edu/huma/illuminations/kell28.htm.

30. Best and Kellner, "Postmodern politics and the battle for the future."

31. John D. Caputo, "Jacques Derrida (1930–2004)," *Journal for Cultural and Religious Theory, Vol. 6*, No. 1 (December 2004): 8.

32. Kristeva, *Intimate Revolt*, 225.

33. Sigmund Freud, *Civilization and Its Discontents*, trans. and ed. James Strachey (New York: W. W. Norton, 1961), 49–50.

34. Kristeva, *Intimate Revolt*, 226.

35. Freud, *Civilization and Its Discontents*, 41.

36. Freud, *Civilization and Its Discontents*, 38.

37. Kristeva, *Intimate Revolt*, 228.

38. Kristeva, *Intimate Revolt*, 230.

39. Kristeva, *Intimate Revolt*, 230.

40. Paul Ricoeur, *Freud and Philosophy: An Essay on Interpretation*, trans. Denis Savage (New Haven: Yale University Press, 1970/1965).

41. Kristeva, *Intimate Revolt*, 230.

42. Kristeva, *Intimate Revolt*, 230–31.

43. Kristeva, *Intimate Revolt*, 234, my emphasis.

44. Kristeva, *Intimate Revolt*, 234.

45. See Kristeva, "What Revolt Today?" in *The Sense and Non-Sense of Revolt: The Powers and Limits of Psychoanalysis, Vol. 1*, trans. Jeanine Herman (New York: Columbia University Press, 2000), 1–2.

46. Kristeva, *Intimate Revolt*, 238.

47. Kristeva, *Intimate Revolt*, 237.

48. M. Jacqui Alexander, *Pedagogies of Crossing: Meditations on Feminism, Sexual Politics, Memory, and the Sacred* (Durham, NC: Duke University Press, 2005), 106.

49. Alexander, *Pedagogies of Crossing*, 106–107.

50. See "The Being of Dasein as Care" in *Being and Time*.

Chapter Three

Freedom-Work

Since we have been arguing that education in its best sense must be linked with the conception of freedom, in this chapter let us investigate how to define freedom. I understand freedom (with the assistance of philosophers Kristeva and Marcuse) as a *goal* or *a project*—something that can be constructed over time and with the assistance and solidarity of others. I do not understand freedom as *a given aspect* of the individual that always already exists and can be uncovered when we peel away the layers of oppression around it. Rather than "freedom-as-kernel," I understand "freedom-as-project." Freedom-as-project is something that (a) is never complete or absolute, (b) never exists apart/separate from others, and (c) we might attain given *maturity* (in the psychoanalytic sense) and *education* (in the Marcusian sense).

The second of these points (i.e., that freedom never exists apart/separate from others) was discussed in the previous chapter on "Radical Teaching." To briefly reiterate that point, I argue from two fronts, *education and psychoanalysis.* On education, I argued against a conception of education as an accumulation of facts that *matter to* and *prepare us for* the present state of (unquestioned) affairs and values, and in favor of an "antinormativist" education that may be provoked in the greatest sense through study in the humanities. M. Jacqui Alexander compares the economy and the academy. One manner of comparison is that "universities provide workers for the economy."[1] And she writes that the "ideological attack" against multiculturalism and feminism makes a statement about "the kind of worker that the transnational empire requires—a worker who fits into an already assigned place within the productive process, without a critical examination of how she got there and who is there with her."[2] On psychoanalysis, I argued that if psychoanalysis works, it puts the subject into a constant state of rebirth. This is a rebirth of the subject not internally so that one could be free *from* others, but one that creates freedom to internalize the outside and engages *with* others. We seek a mature subject free from acting defensively toward the outside world, toward the community. Kristeva writes that psychoanalysis can open up the "plurality of an individual's capacity for connection."[3] I suggested earlier that freedom is not a given, but a *goal*; it is to be *built*. Alongside Kristeva, I contend that this freedom is never built apart from others and in opposition to them, but in concert with them and with their assistance. Others help me (and I can choose to help them), remove my/their/our blocks toward openness per se.

Given this definition of freedom, who are the people who work for freedom? Here I argue that the "freedom-workers" of any given society are those who help to foster in others the aspirations of maturity and education. Utilizing Althusser's conceptions of the "Ideological State Apparatuses," (ISAs) and of "reading" I demonstrate that educators who are freedom-workers are those who inspire us to *read* in the Althusserian sense. This will necessarily involve notions of "the public" because for Althusser, any theory that begins with the notion of the individual is bourgeois and can only end in liberalism. He deems such theories "the fetishism of 'man.'"[4]

ALTHUSSER'S LEVELS OF CLASS STRUGGLE

In his work on "Ideology and Ideological State Apparatuses," Althusser describes three levels at which class struggle takes place: (1) economics, (2) politics, and (3) theory. All people of all classes do carry out all three activities—unwittingly or not. (This is similar to the idea that all people have a philosophy, they just might not be aware of it.) As Hegel says, one must objectify one's idea or philosophy in order to reflect upon it. The same could be said of our practicing of the other two fields, economics and politics—we all do them, but we are not all consciously aware of *how* we do them and thus have not objectified our practices. When practiced with class consciousness, all three levels are effective in the struggle.

Because philosophy is something that everyone does, everyone should do it with class consciousness. This is why philosophy—even more than most disciplines—should avoid specialist lingo, which is a way of speaking only to *one another* in the "ivory tower"—something only other professional and formally-educated philosophers will understand. This is elitist philosophy by definition. It is partly what marks philosophy as different from, say, physics. Both may have specialist jargon, but philosophy has to have an "everyday" jargon as well, because everyday people always already do philosophy. Two statements from Althusser, taken together, make my point. In his piece on ideology, "Reply to John Lewis (Self-Criticism)," he writes, (1) "I will try to speak plainly and clearly, in a way that can be understood by all our comrades;"[5] and, (2) *"philosophy is, in the last instance, class struggle in the field of theory."*[6] These two quotes taken together, place philosophy clearly *in* the public realm, *for* the public realm. It is important for philosophers, economists and politicians to practice in such a way that society in general can benefit from their analyses and practices.

Althusser asserts, "one cannot *begin* with man"[7]—that is bourgeois. Marxism starts from the *economically given social period* and, at the end of analysis, *may* arrive at man. Society is not composed of "individuals."[8] This Althusserian idea resonates with my idea that freedom is not something we can begin with but is something which we must build in society. Indeed, if we are to be on the side of liberation against oppression, then we are necessarily fighting for the freedom of others. When seen in this light, the projects of "human rights" and "liberation" actually seem to be at odds. Clearly, I fall on the side of arguing that liberation is more important than rights. Rights only make sense if individuals exist. I hold that that individuals never exist as "individuals" (a common enough thread in poststructuralist philosophy—the "death of the subject," etc. See for example, Iris Marion Young).

Freedom-work is work that seeks to create liberated persons and societies where we might even be able to recognize something like "rights." If we talk about "rights" before "liberation," then we end up in the quandary that Althusser describes—defending bourgeois ideas. As Young so clearly states, "The philosopher is always socially situated, and if the society is divided by oppressions, she either reinforces or struggles against them."[9] People who fight for rights may (paradoxically) allow oppression to exist because they defend the bourgeois conception of the self. Now some may argue that "human rights" are minimal shields that protect people from the *worst evils* and are not necessarily the best way to achieve the best society. Such philosophers might claim that I am arguing at cross purposes here: a human rights philosopher is fighting against the *worst evils*, whereas the liberationist is fighting for the *best (most moral) society*—that we need not choose between the two. I reluctantly grant this point, even though I am wary to do so.

Furthermore, while at one level, it is true that "rights" often start where the worst infractions occur, looking deeper renders the picture less clear: We see that we may be just as likely to found a society where so-called rights abuses are alleviated or quelled, if we fight from the other side, the side of the "best" society, rather than preventing the "worst." Were we to grant that "rights" are minimal political goods, *we should still not define "freedom" with regards to such rights.* Freedom workers are not those who defend some persons *from* other persons. We can never be free *from* others; we can be free *with* them.

ALTHUSSER ON THE SCHOOL

Althusser claims that in order to continue the present state of affairs (capitalism), we must reproduce the "means of production." This implies not only ensuring that worn-out machinery is replaced or fixed or that buildings are kept-up, but also that *workers* are "kept-up" or "replaced." Althusser writes that this "reproduction of labour power takes place essentially outside the firm."[10] That is, a minimal wage keeps the workers' bellies full while housing and protection from the elements keeps them rested and warm so that they have the energy to work the next day. But also, Althusser says, labour power "must be 'competent,' i.e., suitable to be set to work in a complex system of the process of production."[11] Such job preparation is "decreasingly to be provided for 'on the spot.'"[12] There must be other capitalist institutions that prepare workers for the system that they will find at work. Students learn the "know how" at school but also learn "the 'rules' of good behavior, i.e. the attitude that should be observed."[13]

A clear example of this is "Ethics" as it is often taught in preprofessional programs and—all too commonly—even within philosophy departments. Many ethics courses merely teach the codes of acceptable behavior required for a system to work without disturbance. Even when one discusses "whistle blowing" or some such limit cases, it is often with regards to preserving the overall system, where the goal is not to question the system *too deeply*. In this way, ethics as it is often taught in universities across the country, performs just the function that Althusser claims: teaching and learning the rules of good behavior so that the system works unimpeded. He writes,

> To put this more scientifically, I shall say that the reproduction of labour power requires not only a reproduction of its skills, but also, at the same time, a reproduction of its submission to the rules of established order, i.e. a reproduction of submission to the ruling ideology for the workers . . . so that they, too, will provide for the domination of the ruling class "in words."[14]

Let me put it this way: Fellow academics, we are serving the CEOs and shareholders of companies to which we send our students. They thank us for our cooperation. Our students must be "'steeped' in this ideology in order to perform their tasks 'conscientiously.'"[15] Just as "The State" "is a 'machine' of repression which enables the ruling classes . . . to ensure their domination over the working class,"[16] so does "The School" (as an "ideological state apparatus" or ISA) provide the correct attitude, language, and justifications for such domination. In fact, Althusser claims that of all of the ISAs (like religion, family, media, culture), The School or "education ISA" has the most power in contemporary society. He writes, "Nevertheless, in this concert, one [ISA] certainly has the dominant role, although hardly anyone lends an ear to its music: it is so silent! *This is the School.*"[17]

Althusser does not paint a pretty picture. But he does leave room for subversion:

> I ask the pardon of those teachers who, in dreadful conditions, attempt to turn the few weapons they can find in the history and learning they "teach" *against the ideology*, the system and the practices in which they are trapped. They are a kind of hero. But they are rare and how many (the majority) do not even begin to suspect the "work" the system . . . forces them to do, or worse, put all their heart and ingenuity into performing it with the most advanced awareness (the famous new methods!). So little do they suspect it that their own devotion *contributes* to the maintenance and nourishment of this ideological representation of the School.[18]

ALTHUSSER ON "READING"

Where do we go from here? How do we become the kind of "freedom-workers" that I propose and incite, if Althusser is correct about the obstacles that stand in our way? We are well acquainted with the Enlightenment idea that "education liberates." Not true, says Althusser. Most education in the contemporary world is *anti-liberatory*. In another work, one written five years prior his work on ISAs (The ISA article is from 1970, whereas "From *Capital* to Marx's Philosophy" is from 1965), he elaborates his concept of "reading."

To quickly summarize, ideology is what we live in and through. We can never escape it. But once we recognize that we do live within an ideology, this recognition "unsticks" us from its power to a certain degree. This "unsticking" allows us to *objectify our ideology*, which is precisely when we can begin to *read*. In the ISA piece from which I just quoted heavily, Althusser asserts,

> That is why those who are in ideology believe themselves by definition outside ideology: one of the effects of ideology is the practical *denegation* of the ideological character of ideology by ideology: ideology never says, "I am ideological." It is necessary to be outside ideology, i.e. in scientific knowledge, to be able to say: I am in ideology.[19]

In the earlier piece, "From *Capital*," he writes, "there is no such thing as an innocent reading, we must say what reading we are guilty of."[20] In other words, no one escapes ideological formation, we are all instantiated within an ideology and we do not "absolve" our crime by "confessing it."[21]

Althusser thanks Freud for teaching us a new science of listening and Spinoza and Marx for teaching us a new science of reading.[22] Marx teaches and practices *against "a certain idea of reading which makes a written discourse the immediate transparency of the true."*[23] It is when we break with realism that a new form of discourse occurs, and then (what Althusser calls) "science" can take place. According to Althusser, science—counter-intuitively—is our break with fetishizing reality. Words, images, sounds all require interpretation, and that interpretation always already happens within an ideology—no seeing is "pure seeing"—to believe in "pure seeing" is *precisely* to live inside of an ideology. An analogy to Freud is appropriate: Freud taught us that we must not only listen to the words that people say, but to interpret those words, to listen to where the unconscious speaks. When we truly learn to "read," we are doing the same thing—not accepting something at face value, but reading for the oversights, (e.g., reading for what is hidden, buried, invisible). Only then can "science" become possible. Science end-lessly disrupts ideology. In her article on Althusser's conception of "reading" (a concept she argues has been largely ignored), Ellen Rooney writes,

> To read, for Althusser, is to undertake a political task, that of seeking (produc-ing) alignments and marking exclusions, through close attention to the form of a text's "problematic." Explicitly rejecting what he calls "fetishism," Althusser proposes an account of reading as a guilty, dynamic, flawed, open-ended, historically contingent, and wholly political practice of displacements: *reading as antifetishism.* Finally, in his model, reading is the activity that keeps "sci-ence" alive, where science is understood as the continuous and "endless" project of disrupting ideologies. [24]

CONCLUSION

So, in the end, my conception of "freedom-work" at one level owes some-thing to Enlightenment-thinking—that is: education will liberate us, encour-age people to think for themselves, and so forth. But I also wish to move past this notion. Unlike Enlightenment thought, I do not claim that individuals exist, much less are free in some moment ontologically prior to that libera-tion, nor do I insist on some kind of autonomous authenticity as Heidegger or Sartre might desire. Rather, taking my cues from Althusser on reading, I hope that education is a moment in helping us to learn together the kind of freedom we can experience for connection. Thus, freedom-workers are those who, in Althusser's sense, teach us to read.

NOTES

1. Alexander, Jacqui M., *Pedagogies of Crossing*, (Durham, NC: Duke University Press, 2005) 106.
2. Alexander, *Pedagogies of Crossing*, 106–107.
3. Kristeva, *Intimate Revolt*, 234.

4. Louis Althusser, "Reply to John Lewis," in *On Ideology* (New York: Verso Books, 2008), 84.

5. Althusser, "Reply to John Lewis," 70.

6. Althusser, "Reply to John Lewis." 69.

7. Althusser, "Reply to John Lewis," 85.

8. Althusser, "Reply to John Lewis," 86.

9. Iris Marion Young, *Justice and the Politics of Difference* (Princeton, NJ: Princeton University Press, 1990), 5.

10. Louis, Althusser, "Ideology and Ideological State Apparatuses: Notes towards an Investigation," in *Lenin and Philosophy and Other Essays*, trans. Ben Brewster (New York: Monthly Review Press, 2001), 87.

11. Althusser, "Ideology and Ideological State Apparatuses," 88.

12. Althusser, "Ideology and Ideological State Apparatuses," 88.

13. Althusser, "Ideology and Ideological State Apparatuses," 89.

14. Althusser, "Ideology and Ideological State Apparatuses," 89.

15. Althusser, "Ideology and Ideological State Apparatuses," 89.

16. Althusser, "Ideology and Ideological State Apparatuses," 92.

17. Althusser, "Ideology and Ideological State Apparatuses," 104, my emphasis.

18. Althusser, "Ideology and Ideological State Apparatuses,"106, my emphasis.

19. Althusser, "Ideology and Ideological State Apparatuses," 118.

20. Loius Althusser and Étienne Balibar, "From *Capital* to Marx's Philosophy" in *Reading Capital,* trans. Ben Brewster (New York: Verso Books, 2009), 14.

21. Althusser and Balibar, *Reading Capital*, 15.

22. See Althusser and Balibar, *Reading Capital*, 16–17.

23. Althusser and Balibar, *Reading Capital*, 17, my emphasis.

24. Ellen Rooney, "Better Read Than Dead: Althusser and the Fetish of Ideology," in *Yale French Studies*, No. 88 (1995), 183–200.

Chapter Four

Critically Thinking About
What "Critical Thinking" Is

Two previous chapters directly incite what is taken up here. In chapter 2, we explored James G. Hart's idea that within the contemporary university, the humanities contain the most potential for provoking an *epoché*. I now want to focus our attention on a concept allied to *epoché*, a concept much used and abused in higher education today: *critical thinking*. In chapter 3, I argued that appreciating Althusser's notion of "reading" can help universities to become sites of liberation and a "new university Enlightenment" (as Derrida would say).[1] As argued earlier, what goes on in universities today has little to do with either liberation or enlightenment. Rather, what higher education primarily seeks to do today is to prepare people for the current state of hegemonic affairs, to obtain and efficiently perform a job within the structure. In Althusser's terminology, higher education reproduces the classes and class relationships of the present day. In this chapter, as an aspect of seeking a more precise definition of *critical thinking*, I want to define what kinds of studies in which fashion would constitute a *reading against ideology*, thus preparing people, broadly speaking, for life—a life that includes meaningful work, for sure, but an education that is not limited to job preparation.

We must critically think about what "critical thinking" itself is. Critically thinking requires that we objectify concepts—that we reflect on how we use a particular concept, how others use it, whose interests it serves to use it in various ways, and which direction we would like to take it. This is a Deleuzian task, since he defines philosophy as that branch of intellectual work that overtly invents and reinvents concepts. (In fact, before Deleuze, Socrates also identified philosophy's task as one of defining foundational concepts— justice, love, piety—as a way to newly understand and thus change the world.) But the words and concepts that we already do use are never stagnant in meaning. Therefore, we are in a constant process of redefinition. This redefinition is *always political* to some degree, which is to say: the way that we define key concepts will serve some people and projects up against other people and projects. Most of the time, this redefinition is not overt but covert (more will be said on this later). The concept of "critical thinking" is no different from other key concepts in this way.

Now, in recent times, the use of the concept "critical thinking" has exploded. As an example, at my own university, we added the concept to our mission statement this year, and our college president referred to it in his most recent graduation address (making the bold proclamation that everyone who graduates from our college has been armed with "critical thinking" skills). The phrase has gone from being a set of formal studies within the field of philosophy, mostly associated with the study of logic, to going mainstream and being used widely by assessment leaders, university administrators, corporate and business leaders, and so forth. Because this is the case— that this concept has gone from being used in a specific/narrow sense to a generic/broad sense—it is relevant to look at why and where this has occurred, and who or what projects are served by doing so. We must ask, what *work* is this concept doing for its new users? Who is this use serving and disserving? That is part of my task here. I will argue that there are *three necessary aspects* of critical thinking.

Becoming more open-minded (and thus, being learners per se) requires that we objectify —in order to really see—the ideology in which we live. This is the first aspect of critical thinking: learning how to objectify one's own view of the world. In my undergraduate classes, when describing this idea to students, I have often used an "oatmeal metaphor." I must warn you—it is a crude metaphor, but students seem to respond to it well. It goes something like this: Imagine that we are all born into a big pot of oatmeal. When you live and breathe in that thick, viscous, sweet pot of oatmeal, it is hard to actually *see* the oatmeal or understand your own reality as existing within this oatmeal. You cannot see the oatmeal for what it is because you are inside it. If the woman swimming next to you told you that you were both in oatmeal, you wouldn't believe her. Ideology is like this: when you are deep in it, you cannot see it. (I did promise you that the metaphor would be bad!) This is a way of expressing the idea that recognizing one's own perspective is difficult. Also, this recognition does not come naturally or obviously but must be consciously and continuously labored over. In Sophie Fiennes's recent (2013) movie about ideology, when analyzing the movie *They Live!*, Žižek explains that many people think of ideology as something extra that we learn in life, kind of like brainwashing: our minds are born true and right but then society somehow puts fuzzy glasses on our heads that make us see everything in a "twisted" (ideological) manner.[2]

Žižek says (and I agree) that this common view of ideology is wrong: living in ideology is our *natural state*. We have to encounter persons who help us find the 'glasses' in order to recognize the ideology around us (and in us). Or to put it another way, we are born in and live inside the oatmeal and we don't know it; it is only through conscientious work that we even recognize that there is a pot of oatmeal. There is no purely neutral bystander towering above all of the pots of oatmeal.

What do I mean by this—that there is no neutrality? Many people would have us believe that we can work, vote, consume, love, raise children, eat, read . . . all without philosophy (or broadly more construed: "theory"). This is simply not possible. All action and perception is intertwined with particular sets of ideas (theories/philosophies), though we may not be consciously aware of what that "theory" or "philosophy" is. Believing that one lives one's life *without* or *aside from* philosophy is to live in ideology. That is, one *is* always carrying out a particular philosophy but without always being able to see it for what it is.[3] If you cannot see your own perspective, you cannot critique or change it. In this way, an ideology is a philosophy, but a pre-reflective philosophy. Thus, believing that we can be "neutral" with regards to philosophy means that we—by default—serve status quo ideology. We cannot move into a "new" world (a "new" theory) without understanding and critiquing the one of which we are a part. This begins with the admission that we all live inside philosophies (i.e., there is no neutral), and we must try to deconstruct where we are. As Paulo Freire says, "Conscientization is viable only because consciousness, although conditioned, can recognize that it is conditioned."[4]

On the other hand, let us quickly add, no one is so deeply immersed in ideology that objectification becomes impossible. Here I agree with Terry Eagleton when he writes,

> The critique of ideology, then, presumes that nobody is ever *wholly* mystified. . . . If it rejects the external standpoint of Enlightenment rationality, it shares with the Enlightenment this fundamental trust in the moderately rational nature of human beings. Someone who was entirely the victim of ideological delusion would not even be able to recognize an emancipatory claim upon them; and it is because people do not cease to desire, struggle and imagine, even in the most apparently unpropitious of conditions, that the practice of political emancipation is a genuine possibility.[5]

So far I have described the first aspect of critical thinking. Let us call this (1) *objectifying* the view in which we live and perceive through. We now move on to *the two other aspects of critical thinking*. Critical thinking, as it is most often used, has at least two other meanings: (2) critical thinking as *logic*, and (3) critical thinking as *uncovering*.

(2) Critical thinking as *logic:* Critical thinking is the practice of rationally analyzing expression (spoken or written), and evaluating reasoning in such a way that expressions are broken down into their components and logically analyzed. This aspect of critical thinking requires that one do some disciplined study of logic and rhetoric, which used to be key components to a liberal arts education in the "trivium" (the three parts being grammar, rhetoric, and logic). This manner of understanding of critical thinking stems from Greek philosophy, in particular Aristotle, but also many others.

(3) Critical thinking as *uncovering:* Critical thinking as the practice of uncovering presumptions and power relations. This use of critical thinking necessarily has political ramifications because all ways of seeing and knowing the world are intertwined with power, with who has privilege with regards to particular systems in which ways and who does not. Therefore this way of understanding critical thinking has ties to radical democracy. This arm of critical thinking stems from Marxism, Foucault, and especially the critical theory philosophers of the twentieth century. But this aspect of critical thinking also has strong roots in Plato's dialogues.

To return to the second aspect, I maintain that critical thinking as logical analysis—the most traditional manner of defining critical thinking—is necessary but not sufficient on its own. Only a few decades ago, if one referred to a critical thinking course or textbook, one meant a course or book on logic. I do want to uphold this meaning of the phrase because recent uses have become too slack and often do not include any disciplined study of logic whatsoever. For instance, I teach informal logic in all of my introductory courses in philosophy, though it is not a requirement in my department. I mention this only to underline the fact that I do believe that a basic grasp of logic is necessary to critically thinking; I do not want readers to think that I too quickly deride its usefulness. In particular, I believe that a basic grasp of informal logic—including being able to recognize informal fallacies—is crucial to any education. Ideally this would be taught in high school and then revisited in one's university education. Logic, indeed, helps us to recognize the poor reasoning and attempts at persuasion that surround us daily.

Nonetheless, logic is merely one of three necessary aspects of critical thinking. Derrida explains why rational analysis on its own is insufficient when he writes, "For the principle of reason may have obscurantist and nihilist effects," and a university should be asking questions at a deep level about who and what rationality serves.[6] A university should be a "community of thinking in the broad sense," and not merely a community of research or community of reason. A university built upon being a community of thought "would interrogate the essence of reason and of the principle of reason, the values of the basic, of the principle, of radicality . . . and it would attempt to draw out all the possible consequences of this questioning."[7] "This thinking must also unmask—an infinite task—all the ruses of end-orienting reason" and must interrogate *"apparently disinterested* research."[8] All in all, Derrida describes this new university—where *thinking* is put front and center—as a "new training that will prepare students to undertake new analyses in order to evaluate these ends and to choose, when possible, among them all."[9] This is indeed what Derrida calls a "new university Enlightenment."[10]

In short, if what one means by critical thinking is learning the rules of rational expression, a term synonymous with "logic"—then I agree that is part of critically educating our students, but in itself it will not provoke students to be critical thinkers. Rather, they might just wield a limited tool; able only to critique others when they commit some logical fallacy, but not able to think about what they are doing, why it is relevant, who and what power it serves and why. To get to a deeper level of analysis—more fully "critical" and more fully "thinking"—we need also the first and third aspects of critical thinking. Also, as de Beauvoir writes in *The Ethics of Ambiguity*, logical analysis is never completely objective and there is a danger in thinking that it is: "the critic defines himself positively as the independence of the mind. . . . Thus, he thinks that he himself escapes all earthly criticism. . . . But ambiguity is at the heart of his very attitude, for the independent man is still a man with his particular situation in the world, and what he defines as objective truth is the object of his own choice."[11] If I am the "rational" one who "objectively" holds all truth, then I am deaf to the appeals of others. It is all too easy for me to deem them as irrational and thus not worth my time. No society of justice can be sought where we are deaf to the appeals from others. Let us now move to discussing the third aspect—*critical thinking as uncovering*.

Before I delve too deeply into defining this third aspect, I would like to invoke an article written by Eric Kerl on anarchist studies. Here, Kerl distinguishes two types of anarchist activity: (1) there are those who protest, and (2) there are those who protest but who also study and come to know deeply the bases of their action and how they apply to society, to the past, to various groups of those with and without power, and to various theories. Kerl demonstrates that those in the first group (anarchists who merely protest) do not have a long-term commitment to the project. Speaking with regards to the Occupy movement, he claims that the anarchists of the first group seem to show up at one or two events and then lose interest. Kerl's claim is that such persons may not see how their action and thoughts link them to other places, people, and times. They do not have a structural understanding of why they do what they do, why they think, and what they think, why others think differently. This means their commitment is fleeting, mercurial.[12]

Kerl's analysis of anarchist movements in the 1990s shows how "street tactics" "fostered an atmosphere hostile to political debate" and he quotes the work of Staughton Lynd, who wrote that in the late 1990s that anarchism had a rhetoric, not a theory, and "I am worried that in the absence of theory, many of those who protest in the streets today may turn out to be sprinters rather than long-distance runners."[13] From that Kerl concludes that there has been an "evolving emphasis on practice over theory" and that this poses two problems for anarchism: (1) "the tactic itself became the goal" and (2) this is "a retreat from any goals-based, long-term strategy."[14] He gives the example of "occupy everything, demand nothing" protests—which Kerl says will never work because these anarchists championed "excitement" and "the power that we all find in one another" and remain "unaccountable and representing only themselves and so could not fortunate a coherent set of demands."[15] This, he concludes, is going to be an ineffectual way for moving forward. A movement needs long-term goals and theory. Doing "theory" includes uncovering and laying bare the power relations and presumptions in ways of being and perceiving.

In the same way, I would argue that just teaching our students interesting stories, attractively novel theories about language, beautiful pieces of art, great films, poems, and so forth, divorced from theory—from understanding not just the *what* but also the *why* and the *according to what material conditions and systems of power*, will not make our students critical thinkers. For instance, when students begin to see the ground from which an artwork springs, when they start to see which goals this might limit, which material conditions made it possible, when they understand that the artist had a gender and a race and a class, that certain systems in a given culture made it possible that they be recognized as artists, that they had the privilege to receive the education and support (material and nonmaterial) to perceive themselves as creative persons—it is only then that they begin to understanding that no work exists outside this web, and that to teach or read a work of art (or any work) outside of this web is disingenuous and irresponsible.

Likewise, to suggest in higher education that we want to produce people of action, people who will perform their jobs efficiently and skillfully but who may not understand how their job relates to people on the other side of the globe, to political and economic systems, to the suffering of animals, to global warming, to future or past societies, to structural oppression, or to very particular ways of perceiving and understanding the world, is not to really prepare them for their world or their work at all. It is to prepare them to be doers and not thinkers. It is also to expect them to live lives of alienation.[16] It is not responsible education, and certainly not critical education.[17]

Now that we have covered all three aspects of critical thinking, I want to speak more about the dichotomy between theory and practice—sometimes deemed the difference between "action" and "reflection." This false dichotomy bears directly on the use of critical thinking and particularly to this third aspect of uncovering power relations. We should consider at least two points here:

1. Our current capitalist culture and those who benefit (greatly) from it have a vested interest in getting us to believe that "action" and "reflection" *can* be separated. The system wants all action and no reflection. Because if we reflect on our situation in a broad way, that might just provoke some crazy ideas about fairness, exploitation, and demanding fulfilling lives and work. Best that we be obedient and skillful workers—that is "actors" and not "reflectors." And as college professors and administrators, the system prefers that we prepare those "active laborers" for the system. Not thinkers and reflectors, or, if they do reflect and think—please!—only with regards to efficient completion of the task in front of them!

2. Circumstances of birth, religion, or culture might allow or even force one to understand one kind of injustice. For instance, one might be Dalit in India or Palestinian in Israel and understand injustice due to *caste or race*, but not understand injustice due to *sexuality;* or one might grow up within a religion that calls attention to the injustice of *poverty*, but not really understand injustice due to *gender*. (I would not be the first person to critique the Catholic Church for this; for example, see the work from "Nuns on the Bus").[18] Without theory and reflection—without broad critical thinking in a philosophical way— one will not understand all of the types of oppression and injustice that plague our world.

One clarification: I am not arguing that all philosophy takes place within philosophy courses or even within institutionalized education. For example, I know of some colleagues in our departments of English and Management who use some philosophy/theory in their courses. They don't just teach the required systems, methods, and techniques of their disciplines, but they inspire questions such as, "Why this system, why not another?" "Why is this being or species considered worthy of respect, and not this other being or species?" "Who does this technique serve?" and other critical questions. I've also heard quite a bit of complex theorizing on the streets amongst the best organizers at Occupy rallies, Black Lives Matter protests, Raise the Minimum Wage demonstrations, and so forth. So, when I say that philosophy is required for critical thinking and to inspire long-term commitment to the cause of justice through uncovering power, I do not imply that it can only be practiced by people who have had *formal courses* completed within philosophy departments. In fact, the reverse is also true: I know many students and even professors within departments of philosophy who are sadly lacking in reflection about the world in which they live, especially with regards to issues of oppression. We've all heard of professional philosophers who claim, for instance, that feminism is not "real" philosophy. This is the kind of antireflection to which I'm referring. Professional philosophy can become a

kind of clever puzzle solving—fun and intellectually stimulating—but hardly
aware of or reflective upon the ground from which it stems and the oppression in which it participates. So, let us be clear that I believe that philosophy
is *not limited* to philosophy departments, nor does everyone *within the
bounds* of that department practice philosophy as broad, critical reflection.

In his work, *Cultural Action for Freedom*, Freire also warns against separating action and reflection. He knows that language and thought are tied
together; he writes, "the human word is more than mere vocabulary—it is
word-and-action . . . *speaking the word* really means: a human act implying
reflection and action." [19] "For the learner to know what he did not know
before, he must engage in an authentic process of *abstraction* . . . on [the]
forms of orientation in the world." [20] In sum, theory of knowing and a method
have to go together "as an aspect of knowing, learning to read and write
presupposes not only a theory of knowing but a method that corresponds to
the theory." [21] Freire recognizes that subjectivity and objectivity are always
entwined. "Reality is never just simply objective datum, the concrete fact,
but always men's perception of it" [22] and "the learners gradually, hesitatingly,
and timorously place in doubt the opinion they held of reality." [23]

I have noticed this happening in particular in any class where I teach
feminism. And it occurs, in my experience, with female and male students
equally. Once we start deconstructing and questioning gender roles, it is as if
they are seeing reality anew by discovering the reasons underlying many of
their own attitudes. It happens every semester and it happens with the majority of the class, even when I am teaching feminism in an Introduction to
Philosophy class. I think feminism is such a strong case of what Freire
describes because most people, by the age of nineteen or twenty, have been
acting out gender roles every day of their lives. Perhaps they have been
frustrated here or there—but they lack concepts and theories for thinking
about what to do with their frustration and in fact, much of that frustration is
unconscious and cries out for explanation and analysis.

Something similar happens when I show the movie *Earthlings* in my
Justice classes. [24] Many students have had semiconscious feelings of guilt
about the ways in which they suspect that animals are treated in factory
farming. Most have also had some loving relationships with animals in their
families (such as cats or dogs), and subconsciously, they sense the contradiction in treating dogs one way and pigs another. Then they learn through the
movie that the "gritty reality" of factory farming, animal testing, the fur/
leather trade, and so forth. is worse than they could have imagined. [25] Seeing
that footage, however, is not enough. At the same time, we all need concepts,
theories, philosophies, and moral principles in order to frame and discuss this
field. Many students openly sob when they watch this film. But emotion is
not enough. One can have a good cry and then repress it all later, being
alienated from one's own moral principles. [26] (We will further discuss the

role of emotions and passion to critical thinking in the next chapter.) But when these scenes are unpacked, when we analyze events and acts by discussing how and why they occur, how capitalism is implicated, how our own desires are implicated, how our notions of pain and suffering apply, why or how different kinds of violence and oppression are related—everyone in the classroom all of a sudden has the tools and theories for describing their world, for abstracting their reality, making an object of their reality (as Marx would say) and then scrutinizing that object to ask if *that* is really the world that she or he chooses. Critical thinking should be a sledgehammer to bad faith. It says, "Here is your reality. Here are the principles and ideas that govern it; here are others that are missing. Here are those who benefit from the world as it is, and here are those who are oppressed. Now you must choose whether you agree with and can defend this reality and its principles or not." This reality can be the truth of poverty and class war, it can be the truth of racism and sexism, or it can be the truth of factory farming.

Baez and Boyles' 2009 book, *The Politics of Inquiry,* argues from a parallel position that theory is necessary for critical education and for justice. They are concerned with saving theory from those who think that education can be accomplished perfectly well without it. Many behaviorists and positivists (across various departments, but particularly so within the social sciences and within schools of education and business) are *anti-theory.* They claim to want to focus only on data and all matters "practical." But Baez and Boyles rightly point out that all acts of listening, reading, and interpreting the world stem from a theory of the world (or, as indicated earlier, "there is no neutral"). They claim that their project is theoretical *and* practical. Like Jonathan Culler, they believe that theory is necessary to disrupt "common sense." They write, "Inquiry leading to theories, therefore, is 'practical' to the extent it changes people's views, and makes them think differently"[27] and "Theories . . . move across space and time and (re)shape the worlds they touch."[28] What Marcuse wrote in 1960 is even truer today as we face neoliberal notions of educational reforms:

> Since the established universe of discourse is that of an unfree world, dialectical thought is necessarily destructive, and whatever liberation it may bring is liberation in thought, in theory. However, the divorce of thought from action, of theory from practice, is itself part of an unfree world.[29]

And hooks too warns against separating theory and practice: "By reinforcing the idea that there is a split between theory and practice or by creating such a split, both groups deny the power of liberatory education for critical consciousness, thereby perpetuating conditions that reinforce our collective exploitation and repression."[30]

NOTES

1. See Jaques Derrida, "The Principle of Reason" in *Eyes of the University: Right to Philosophy 2*, ed. Werner Hamacher and David E. Wellbery, trans. Jan Plug and Others (Stanford, CA: Stanford University Press, 2004), 132.

2. *The Pervert's Guide to Ideology*, directed by Sophie Fiennes (2012; United Kingdom, 2013), DVD, and the movie Žižek refers to is *They Live!*, directed by John Carpenter (1988; USA, 2003), DVD.

3. An idea garnered or sharpened with the reading of Louis Althusser's work.

4. Paulo Freire, "Cultural Action and Conscientization," *Cultural Action for Freedom* (Cambridge, MA: Harvard Educational Review and The Center for the Study of Development and Social Change, 2000), 41; I changed his sexist language.

5. Terry Eagleton, *Ideology: An Introduction* (New York: Verso Books, 2007), xxiii.

6. Derrida, "The Principle of Reason," 147–48.

7. Derrida, "The Principle of Reason," 148.

8. Derrida, "The Principle of Reason," 148, my emphasis.

9. Derrida, "The Principle of Reason," 148.

10. Derrida, "The Principle of Reason," 132.

11. Simone de Beauvoir, *The Ethics of Ambiguity*, trans. Bernard Frechtman (New York: The Citadel Press, 1964), 68–69.

12. One point that Eric Kerl makes in "Contemporary Anarchism" is that in the 1980s, anarchist ideas "were reduced to a tiny cultural milieu, stripped of virtually all class politics" and instead "emphasized the politics of the personal; veganism, interpersonal relations, and lifestyle choices, rather than revolutionary class politics" (3). I disagree with Kerl that lifestyle choices are not political. Becoming a vegan is a very potent political statement. But, I see his point about how some people attempted their lifestyle choices to be "merely personal." Of course, that is never possible.

13. Eric Kerl, "Contemporary Anarchism" in *International Socialist Review*, Issue # 72, July 2010, http://isreview.org/issue/72/contemporary-anarchism.

14. Kerl, "Contemporary Anarchism."

15. Kerl, "Contemporary Anarchism."

16. More will be said about alienation in chapter 5.

17. Of the three aspects I argue are necessary for critical thinking, one could claim that aspects one (objectification of one's own view) and three (uncovering power relations) are in fact related or the same thing. I considered this view myself and at the 2014 Phenomenology Roundtable, Carolyn Cusick (Fresno State) suggested this point. However, I believe that my case is stronger when aspects one and three are separated as necessary aspects because in both cases, it might be possible to accomplish one without the other. Therefore in order to emphasize the importance of all three aspects, I will keep them separated as minimal requirements for anything that claims to be critical thinking.

18. See, for example, "Solidarity with Sisters," http://solidaritywithsisters.weebly.com/in-the-news.html, or Sister Simone Campbell, S.S.S., "California Catholic" in *A Nun on the Bus: How All of Us Can Create Hope, Change, and Community* (HarperOne, 2014), 8–9.

19. Paulo Freire, "The Adult Literacy Process," *Cultural Action for Freedom*, trans. Loretta Slover (Cambridge, MA: Harvard Educational Review and The Center for the Study of Development and Social Change, 2000), 20.

20. Freire, "Adult Literacy Process," 21.

21. Freire, "Adult Literacy Process," 22.

22. Freire, "Adult Literacy Process," 22.

23. Freire, "Adult Literacy Process," 24.

24. *Earthlings*, directed by Shaun Monson (2005; Nation Earth, 2008), DVD. Available for free online viewing at www.earthlings.com.

25. Teaching students the "gritty reality" of their world is held by some to be one of the key aspects of Jesuit education. In what must be one of the most referenced speeches ever given by a Jesuit, Father Kolvenbach claims that students of Jesuit education should "[L]et the gritty reality of this world into their lives, so they can learn to feel it, think about it critically, respond

to its suffering and engage it constructively . . . [because solidarity with our less fortunate brothers and sisters] is learned through 'contact' rather than through 'concepts.' . . . When the heart is touched by direct experience, the mind may be challenged to change. Personal involvement with innocent suffering, with the degradation and injustice that others suffer, is the catalyst for solidarity which then gives rise to intellectual inquiry, reflection, and action," see Peter-Hans Kolvenbach, S.J, "The Service of Faith and the Promotion of Justice in American Jesuit Higher Education," available from http://www.xavier.edu/jesuitresource/jesuit-a-z/documents/TheServiceofFaithandthePromotionofJusticeinAmericanJesuitHigherEducation--Kolvenbach.pdf.

26. I have in mind here work on alienation by Richard Schmitt, such as *Alienation and Class* (Schenkman Books, Inc., 1983), *Alienation and Social Criticism (Key Concepts in Critical Theory)* (Humanities Press, 1994, cowritten with Thomas E. Moody), and *Alienation and Freedom* (Westview Press, 2003).

27. Benjamin Baez and Deron Boyles, *The Politics of Inquiry: Education Research and the "Culture of Science"* (Albany, NY: State University of New York Press, 2009), viii.

28. Baez and Boyles, *Politics of Inquiry*, viii.

29. Marcuse, 1960, quoted from Henry Giroux, *Theory and Resistance in Education* (Westport: Bergin & Garvey, 2001), 2.

30. bell hooks, *Teaching to Transgress: Education as the Practice of Freedom* (New York: Routledge, 1994), 69.

Chapter Five

Method, bell hooks, and Paulo Freire

Too many contemporary educators stress only the method by which one learns. In universities now, there is an emphasis on skills (writing as a skill, information literacy as a skill, and yes, critical thinking as a skill). But to focus only on the *how* and not on the *what*, risks our falling into what Lewis R. Gordon calls "method fetishism"—that is, when we focus only upon the methods of knowing and assume that this will grant us the highest degree of objectivity aside from content, context or theory.[1] Gordon charges that many philosophers and social scientists don't often (for instance) ask about the experiences of suffering or oppression, but make a fetish out of *how* we get our data, arguing amongst themselves about who does or doesn't have the most rigorous and objective methodology. Directing us to critical work done by Frantz Fanon and W. E. B. Du Bois, Gordon claims that even philosophers who do talk about suffering often do so in terms of distribution methods, not about the people who suffer. Stanley Aronowitz writes that Freire's ideas have largely been reduced to a simple "methodology" by his North American readers, "following a tendency in all the human and social sciences" to be obsessed with methods.[2] I agree with Gordon and Aronowitz that it is not *only method* that matters in education, and that objectivity cannot be the only or primary goal of scholarship (as if it were possible anyway!).

bell hooks sometimes comes close to fetishizing method when she writes about critical thinking. Like Gordon, hooks wants to "decolonize" thought. On that we all should agree. But hooks mistakenly focuses on method as the way of reaching that goal. It is revealing for us to do a close reading of her thinking on this matter: She and I share a similar project (analyzing critical thinking) and a similar goal (education as the practice of freedom). Despite my deep respect for her work, there are several points at which she and I part ways, and this parting is, I think, helpful for us as we try to pin down what is important about critical thinking and how we might fully instantiate it into higher education. In her books *Teaching to Transgress* and *Teaching Critical Thinking,* hooks stresses two key points regarding promoting critical thinking and liberation: (a) "personal experience sharing" in the classroom, and (b) passion in the classroom. From my perspective, neither of these is a sufficient aspect of teaching critical thinking. hooks doesn't think the two, taken separately, are sufficient either. But she does appear to say that taken together, they are enough.

Teaching to Transgress brings up the issue of building a classroom space where we "allow every student to come to voice." hooks believes that encouraging students to find their voice and share their personal experiences will promote critical thinking. Students, she writes, must "find their true voice."[3] It is for this reason that hooks builds her argument that the classroom is a place to get students to give voice to their own personal experiences and for the professor to share her or his own personal experiences. How exactly does this promote critical thinking? Couldn't it be just as likely or more likely that ideology will be given voice? My students recounted to me an anecdote about a fellow professor at my university who spent many days during the semester talking about her boyfriend. One day she excitedly donned a big diamond engagement ring and spent the hour explaining to students how her boyfriend proposed to her. Certainly this is "sharing of personal experiences"—but are we certain that a straight-forward lecture on Marx with no personal experience sharing would have promoted liberatory thinking less than this? Perhaps I've shamelessly committed a straw man fallacy in claiming that hooks would be in favor of professors behaving like this (I'm sure she would not favor such behavior!). But I bring up this example to state that personal experience sharing in the classroom is no guarantee of teaching against ideology. Rather, personal experience sharing can promote or can make students feel safe and secure in their ideology. It is not only that we speak or that students speak; what is *as important* is *what* is said, read, and questioned that promotes critical thinking. As Aronowitz and Giroux write, there is a certain strain of critical pedagogy that "comes perilously close to emulating the liberal-progressive tradition in which teaching is reduced to getting students merely to express or assess their own experiences" and this case, teaching "collapses into a banal notion of facilitation" and "an unproblematic vehicle for self-affirmation."[4] It is not trendy in this academic climate to say it, but content matters. Skills and methods cannot be divorced from content. Therefore, personal experience sharing is neither a sufficient nor a necessary cause for critical thinking in the classroom. Aronowitz says,

Within the United States it is not uncommon for teachers and administrators to say that they are "using" the Freirean method in classrooms. What they mean by this is indeterminate. Sometimes it merely connotes that teachers try to be "interactive" with students; sometimes it signifies an attempt to structure class-time as, in part, a dialogue between the teacher and students; some even mean to "empower" students by permitting them to talk in class. [5]

These practices, however, do not compose the revolutionary impact of Freire's philosophy—in fact, the practices "hardly require Freire as a cover."[6] As McLaren and Leonard say, Freire's ideas are always in danger of becoming "domesticated" and I would argue that limiting the critical impact of his work to a mere classroom methodology is one way that the domestication occurs in the United States.[7] "[W]hat makes education political for Freire is both its content and form and its relationship to the larger economic and social structure."[8]

Let us think about the issue of passion/dispassion as it relates to critical thinking. A more traditional understanding of critical thinking (as tied to logic) does its best to completely rid human expression of passion. As much as rational and irrational are set up in a binary relation, logic is paired with the rational and passion with the irrational. (Nietzsche is in a small club when he states, "Behind all logic and its seeming sovereignty of movement, too, there stand valuations"!)[9] Logic has always been an attempt at escape from the realms of feeling to a "higher" level of thinking. That human expression and thought can be improved by understanding logic, I agree. That through the use of logic we have thereby rid ourselves of the passions, I disagree. However, hooks goes to the opposite extreme in claiming that critical thinking is primarily about passion and personal experience sharing. She frequently says that critical thinking requires that we be passionate: "The most exciting aspect of critical thinking in the classroom is that it calls for initiative from everyone, actively inviting all students to think passionately and to share ideas in a passionate, open manner."[10] I believe that passion doesn't necessarily have anything to do with critical thinking. One can be at the extreme of passionate thinking and be utterly closed-minded. (Think of religious dogmatists who passionately defend their beliefs and won't hear a critical word against them!) In fact, it is more often the case that this willingness to passionately share your personal experiences ("coming to voice") might come from a lack of critical thought, or rather from staunchly defending one's ideology. We all know examples of people who get their hackles up, turn defensive and protective in the most passionate way if their life choices or beliefs have been criticized (or merely questioned). hooks claims that critical thinking *empowers* us as individuals. I'm not so sure. *I think critical thinking deflates us as private and separable individuals and privileged sites of knowing.* To return to my first aspect of critical thinking, the first aspect requires us to objectify our own view. "Coming to voice" or "speaking passionately" without the willingness to objectify one's own view will not lead one to critical thinking.

Another comment about hooks's promotion of "passion" as it links to critical thinking: she equates the "banking system" of education (Freire's term) with a boring education, a boring classroom. She creates a dichotomy between (a) the passionate classroom, which is all about students sharing their personal experiences, which (somehow) promotes critical thinking, and (b) The boring classroom which relies upon teachers lecturing, teaching students content—and which does not promote critical thinking.[11] This dichotomy is unhelpful. Either kind of classroom—the one based primarily on lectures (or as some now deem it, "chalk and talk") or the one based on personal sharing experiences—can promote critical thinking or can remain within the realm of ideological thinking. There are other factors at play here, such as, Which texts are being read? Does the professor link the text to the concrete world? Are there questions raised about the text? Are students encouraged to question their own presumptions about this text, its ideas, its characters, their material conditions, and so forth? Have the professor and the class been encouraged to uncover the "blind spots" of this text? Is the professor him or herself modeling critical, anti-ideological thinking? These questions can be taken up in lecture form or in a circle of discussion. Or they can be glossed over in either form. Again, one must avoid making a fetish of method.

Nothing suggests to me that the method of teaching all by itself is linked to critical thinking. Certainly there are lecture-based courses that fail to inspire or provoke critical thought. The same is true of courses that focus on student participation. The answer lies in the "how" and in the "what" of the course content and in fact on many other factors. Other factors that might lead to a rich experience in the classroom include a small class size, a professor who has intellectual relationships with those students, a professor who reads and evaluates the students' work (rather than having an "underling" do this work!), a professor who has academic freedom and security in her or his position, students who have material lives that allow them the space and rest that they need in order to devote time to study, a surrounding culture that is not dismissive of intellectual concerns, racial and gender oppression absent from the classroom, and many other important factors.

Let us now move backwards in influence to look more closely at one of hooks's main inspirations, Paulo Freire, certainly one of the most if not *the* most important figure in critical pedagogy. Freire is widely read in the United States in both schools of education and in humanities departments. The idea most discussed and associated with him in the United States is his critique of the "banking" conception of knowledge, meant to show that most of how education has been carried out in the past century has emphasized an accumulation and memorization of facts—*data*—and not *thinking*. This idea is not, of course, unique to Freire; Socrates discusses something similar 2,000 years earlier in the *The Republic* when he says that the goal of true education is not the accumulation of facts, but the "turning around of the soul" toward higher-level thinking. [12] Socrates says that there are ways of studying certain subjects that provoke questions in us, and it is this questioning that turns our souls around. This can be accomplished by adopting the position of wonder and curiosity and being open to the world. I think Freire is saying something similar.

I largely agree with and am also deeply inspired by Freire's work. However, I am disconcerted by the manner in which his ideas have been co-opted by most American education theorists. The typical situation is that teachers (or students) use Freire's critique of "banking" education as a simplistic way of saying, "See? We shouldn't be teaching or learning subject matter, ideas, theories, or texts at all. That's all just data in the bank! We should be able to let our minds run free without all of that data!" I completely disagree with this use of Freire's ideas. I also don't think it is in keeping with his overall work.

Freire stresses repeatedly that every type of education has to take the concrete situation of the students into consideration. We need to ask what kind of education we are focusing upon, who are the students and what is their background, what is the economic situation of our area or school—and I would add, though I think it is implied in Freire's work—*what kind of ideology we are working against*. This is all a way of asserting that the professor needs to be aware of context. Freire's context in teaching (mostly) poor, illiterate, more communally minded farmers in Latin America is not at all the same context as (for instance) teaching literate, high school educated, white, middle-class Americans (who are thoroughly inundated with contemporary popular culture and the reign of "individualism"). The context is not the same and so the approach cannot be the same. Why? Because the ideology that we are reading against is not the same. *A materialist approach to critical pedagogy must understand the differences between different contexts.* Freire (as hooks discerns) talks a lot about students taking up the "subject" position. Indeed, this is a requirement for learning to occur. But one cannot only be in a subjective position or there is no space created for learning. Subjective self-absorption is not conducive to learning or to critical thinking. By contrast, I would argue that an honest and critical *oscillation* between subjective and objective is required for learning. Phenomenology helps us to see that none of us operates from a wholly subjective or wholly objective position. [13]

In Jesuit education, we say that the teacher must "meet the student where she or he is" and teach to the "whole person." To believe that all students are the same (and that the same methodology works on all of them—regardless of their "ground") is to engage in dangerous essentialism. If I am correct and the goal of higher education is to get our students to read against their ideology, then the professor must begin by having a deep and thorough understanding of her own culture and the kinds of ideological presumptions that her students are likely to hold. In other words, to be a critical educator, the professor must first and foremost work dialectically.

I take up an example from chapter 1 of *Cultural Action for Freedom*: Freire talks about the books that are used for adult literacy—he is poking fun at the average vocabulary they teach in primers for literacy. He claims, "the authors repeat with the texts what they do with the words, that is, they introduce them into the learners' consciousness as if it were empty space— once more, the 'digestive concept of knowledge'" (this refers to Freire's earlier admonition of those who understand education as "putting food into empty bellies").[14] What Freire writes seems true and appropriate for teaching literacy to adults. This is his context—his ground. But as Freire himself writes, one cannot take some idea from a particular context and apply it willy-nilly to every context.[15] To again refer to Hegel—if the thesis is different, the antithesis has to be different. What is "other" to one culture or situation is not the same "other" of a different culture or situation. This means that as teachers, the first step is to know the thesis—the ground, the culture, from which our students stem. Only then can we know what "other" they need to break them out of their own particular ideology towards liberatory thinking.

I do believe that many of Freire's readers create too strong of a binary between knowing and memorization. Freire writes about the "*radical distinction* between knowing and memorizing."[16] Knowing involves some memorization, though certainly memorization is not enough. It would be most correct to say that memorization is a necessary but not sufficient condition for knowing. But one should *not* interpret Freire (as so many of his readers do) as saying that learning and knowing new material is not important to education. We ourselves are inspired to ideas and thought by knowing other people's ideas. Without the work of others, we ourselves have no work. (In fact, without others, we don't even have a language to express or think our ideas. And as we have learned from contemporary philosophers, language itself creates a vision of the world; when we speak, when we think *through* grammar, we are already within an ideology. Judith Butler's work on gender has forcefully made this point.) We are amongst a community of learners, and we learn best when we know, learn, and understand their ideas. To give a brief example: I once had an undergraduate philosophy major who, as an eighteen-year-old incoming freshman, claimed that he did not want to read or learn "anyone else's philosophy"—he just wanted the space and time to express his own philosophy. Without knowing any ideas from Socrates, Aristotle, Hegel, de Beauvoir, and so forth, he felt ready to express and propound his own philosophy of the world! While I certainly appreciated his courage and tried to inspire him to continue creating his philosophy on his own time, I

also believe that it is arrogant to not see oneself as a member of an intellectual community where we are both listeners and speakers. Thought needs material to be thought. Without learning and seriously considering the ideas of
others, our minds are just turning wheelies. This is a basic Hegelian idea: the
self is only the self when it welcomes/learns/incorporates what is *not-self*—
what is other, what is new, what is antithetical to the self. I believe that Freire
would agree with me on this issue. But many "Freirians" would not.

Freire writes that "we have never rejected positive contributions from
men of the third world or of the director societies. But confrontation with our
particular world has taught us that any ideas coming from another part of the
world cannot simply be transplanted."[17] Ideas cannot simply be transplanted!
Surely Freire would admit that this must be the case for his own ideas as
well—that is, the exact education that works in his context of teaching rural,
illiterate farmers cannot be mimicked and transplanted onto middle-class,
contemporary American university students. In fact, I believe that hooks
makes a mistake herself when she describes how she transplants Freire's
ideas into her classroom. Yet, hooks and Freire both share the idea that (as
Freire writes) "our thinking may coincide historically with the unrest of all
those who . . . are struggling to have a voice of their own."[18]

Again, there is a danger here of slipping into the ideology of the individual, of the modernist belief. Perhaps Freire is being polemical in the culture in
which he lives. Those oppressed often have trouble finding their own voice.
One puts forward a strong "individual" gesture because *that* is what they
need to counterbalance their strong belief in communal (good) but also their
belief that they don't matter. I'm not sure that idea transplants over to
American university students—or at least not to all of them. Americans are
steeped in the ideology of the individual. The polemical gesture for *them* is to
bring forward the communal, the common good, the ways in which we are all
in relation to each other, and the ways in which we are all tied in systemic
fashion that is often oppressive. So, I agree that a polemical gesture is needed
to provoke critical thinking. But this gesture cannot be easily "transplanted"
from one culture to another.

Freire privileges dialogue as the key to true learning. "The educator
whose approach is mere memorization is anti-dialogic"—he asserts. And yet,
he also quickly notes, "not all dialogue is in itself the mark of a relationship
of true knowledge."[19] This reminds me of a counterpoint that I made to
hooks when she claimed that critical thinking and "coming to voice" of
students are necessarily linked. I disagreed by claiming that, actually, it all
depends on *what* is being said in the classroom, which texts are being considered, how questions are being raised, and so forth. Just "coming to voice" in
and of itself is no guarantee of critical thinking, just as Freire says here that
not all dialogue is learning.

On the other hand, there are those who are so very deeply oppressed that they do not believe they have anything to think or say. Freire writes that many of the illiterate laborers had no voice because their lives did not require them to speak: "We only had to carry out orders."[20] This reminds me of a group of poor, Dalit women whom I met in rural India. The most touching moment of our visit arrived when we were sitting in a large room with about a dozen visiting Americans and about twenty to twenty-five women who represented an adult literacy group. These women or their parents used to work in silk sari factories. Because the pay was so low, and because life situations would come up that required far more money than they earned (doctor's visits, weddings, funerals), they would often borrow money from the company. The only way to pay it back was to agree to put one of their own children to work in the factory. The result was that this area of India had a very low literacy rate, especially for women and children who were living as slaves to the sari companies. A group of Indian Catholic nuns came in and slowly began the process of optional education after work hours for the children who worked in the sari factories. Shockingly, even after full days of grueling work, the children would willingly come to evening classes to learn to read, write, paint, and do basic math. Eventually, government officials discovered the child slavery in the area (although according to the women in the village, they probably knew beforehand and found it more convenient to look the other way until it became widely publicized). The result is that many of the women (mothers of the child slaves) learned to read and write too. They then formed their own bank co-op to help one another cover various large life costs. And these women even got themselves elected to local political office. All of this happened within thirteen years! After one of the nuns explained this situation, she asked each of the women to stand and say her name. A simple exercise. But it took a long time as many would burst into giggles, or tear up and look at the floor. Many refused to stand up altogether. The Americans were puzzled. We didn't exactly know what was going on. After this exercise, the nun explained, "These women don't feel that they have a right to say their own names. That is how little they think of themselves. It takes a long time to even get them to say their own names." I believe at that moment, I understood something of what Freire is saying in a way that I never had before. There are people in the world who are so terribly and deeply oppressed that even voicing their own name seems like an absurdity. For this context, I could not agree with Freire more.

However, surely this is not the case with many of our American students currently enrolled in universities, who, if given a chance, will talk about themselves, their fashion likes and dislikes, their beer and pizza preferences, their sports team preferences, and even the body shape they prefer in a sexual partner! Again, different context, different antithesis required. As a materialist, I'm certain that Freire would understand this. As the saying from Jesuit education goes, a teacher has to meet the students where they are. I would add, yes, and we also have to challenge them according to the ground on which they are.

hooks believes that "now more than ever we need critical thinking."[21] Perhaps this is only a rhetorical device on hooks's part. But I'd like to challenge it nonetheless—not the part about how we need critical thinking, but the part about how "now more than ever" we need it: (1) I'm not sure this is true. Surely during the time of slavery, critical thinking would have been useful if more widespread. During times of women's suffrage, it would have been helpful. Yes, we are in a time now too where there is deep and wide-spread oppression due to class, sexuality, gender, and things will get worse because of environmental problems that we seem to be ignoring. But I'm not sure *now* is worse than other times; (2) I claim this critical thinking is impor-tant *to every time and every culture*. Why do I think hook's view is danger-ous? Because it opens the door to say that critical thinking is only needed at certain times and in certain places. Some people (perhaps even the majority) may come to believe that they have everything pretty much figured out and they don't need critique anymore. That is dangerous. This is a claim I hear often regarding feminism, by the way. Many claim that feminism had its time in the past, but now that women have (for example) the right to vote and own property, sexism is over and there is no need for gender critique anymore. When one claims that one time or culture needs critical thinking more than other times or cultures, this attitude is not far way.

In contrast to hooks on this point, I agree more with Judith Suissa's writing on anarchism when she says that the anarchist should see how *con-stant education in critique and questioning* is necessary. She makes an im-portant distinction between (some) Marxists versus (some) anarchists along this line. Some Marxists tend to believe that once the bourgeois revolution occurs, society will be at its ideal. "Once the revolution is over, it seems, there will be no role for education, for as Lukács writes, scientific socialism will then be established."[22] Anarchism, however, requires constant education because (1) human beings always have both the positive and negative qual-ities present and the seeds of a stateless society are present in human moral qualities, but (2) there is no one scientifically correct form of social organiza-tion. So education must be constantly ongoing; it is not about reaching some fixed end-point but about maintaining creative experimentation in keeping with moral values and principles, "to create the conditions of freedom."[23]

Like Suissa, I believe that every era and every culture is in need of critical thinking: (1) Human animals have potentialities to develop social virtues or not. This depends largely upon education (education broadly understood, not just what occurs within "the school"—though the school is an important site, since, as Althusser points out, it is an institution where the majority of young people spend the majority of their time) and (2) like Derrida, I believe that we should always be on the prowl for justice to come and "the university to come." This means that at all times, we have to be open, curious learners— open to the possibility that the way that we perceive or think could be in need of expansion. To find out what is "wrong" and "right" in our own thinking, we require critical thinking. Thus the close relationship between ethics and critical thinking. Both require *listening* in the broad sense of that term.

In Derek Bok's book *Universities on the Marketplace*, he outlines the ways in which market-thinking has pervaded higher education and writes that part of the problem is *vagueness* in our purpose and mission. When our purposes as a university are vague, we can persuade others (and ourselves) that commercialization fits in just fine with our mission. The key concepts of "excellence," "ethics," "interdisciplinarity," the "public," "critical thinking," and many others have been blurred and domesticated to the point of mean- inglessness. We have to insist that our educational institutions be clear on what their missions are and how they use such key concepts. Michael Apple is right: our task as educators is not merely to "prepare students to function easily in the 'business' of [our particular] society. A nation is not a firm. A school is not a part of that firm."[24] Rather, students should be enabled "to inquire as to *why* a particular form of social collectivity exists, *how* it is maintained, and *who* benefits from it."[25] So, what we mean by critical think- ing cannot be merely to teach our students how to find new niches and business opportunities within the framework of today. Nor can it be to mere- ly teach them logic. Or to encourage passion or personal sharing in the classroom.

There is another aspect of the corporatization of higher education that bears upon the issue of teaching and of critical thinking: a certain use of student evaluations that equates students with customers and proclaims that the customer is always right. Don't get me wrong: I believe that student course evaluations are an integral part of the evaluation of faculty. But there is a good use and a poor use of these evaluations. Good use involves asking questions about the professor's availability to the students, the feedback re- ceived, the openness of the classroom dynamic, the clarity of the lectures and assignments. I believe that narrative questions and evaluation do this better than numerical/quantitative scores do. An open-ended essay question such as "Was this professor adept at explaining and clarifying the course material, and if so how and if not why not?" can get remarkably detailed and honest responses from students. Other important questions include: "Was professor present, on time, and prepared for class? In what way could professor prepare for class in more ways?" and, "Was this professor available outside of class during office hours and open to discussion with students?"

Poor use of student evaluations involves multiple choice questions that gauge the popularity of a professor, "On a scale of 1–5, 5 being the highest" rate the professor in the following areas: "Grading and feedback was fair."

For instance, there is a strong correlation between grade inflation and student's "scores" of professors. Some colleges and universities rate the goodness of their professors based solely on the number received on such evaluations, such that a professor who gets a 4.9 is a "better" teacher than a professor who gets a 3.2. This is the exact wrong use of evaluations. It works *against* critical thinking because it may dissuade professors from truly challenging their students. Those with weak egos often experience "challenge" as unfriendly. (Perhaps this is truer only in the short term. We all know stories of people who claim that some of the worst grades they got in classes from some of the hardest professors they had, later on in life admit that those were the best professors they had.) This is especially important because the majority of professors in college and universities today are contingent. They may have an extra impetus to aim for higher student evaluation numbers. At a university where evaluation is done merely by comparing numbers—"4.9 is a better professor than 3.2"—is a serious disservice to critical education.

Part of my goal in this chapter has been to demonstrate that (1) critical thinking is vital to what a university should be, and (2) we need to be clear and specific in defining what critical thinking is. At first glance, it seems that our universities already are committed to teaching critical thinking (the phrase is ubiquitous!). But on closer inspection, we see that universities want the cachet of the traditional meaning of the term *critical thinking* without including the kinds of studies that would encourage it. This is one reason why there seems to be a disjunction in higher education these days between our mission statements and what we actually teach. We want to "have the cake" of a public-focused educational mission, but we want to "eat the cake" of business-driven, market-based decisions and bankrolls. It is clear that modern academia is guilty of institutional hypocrisy.

NOTES

1. Gordon presented these ideas at the *Radical Philosophy Association* conference in October, 2012. Works of his that explore similar issues include "Manifesto of Transdisciplinarity. Not to become slaves of the knowledge of others," in *Trans-pasando Fronteras*, No 1 (2011), https://www.icesi.edu.co/revistas/index.php/trans-pasando_fronteras/rt/printerFriendly/1289/1755, where Gordon states,

> There is another type of epistemological colonization. There is colonization on the level of methods. It deals with not only colonization of *what* one thinks but also with *how* one thinks. So we find these practices alive in the scenarios of what I call disciplinary decadence. This is when a discipline turns away from what gives it life. This is what it means to decay, to die. One form of that decadence is methodological fetishism and fetishizing methods. This is where a scholar or a student may study something, work hard on it, bring it to a community of scholars, and the others are only interested in the methods. They are not interested in whether the findings or argument is true or have any bearing on reality.

2. Stanley Aronowitz, "Paulo Freire's Radical Democratic Humanism," in *Paulo Freire: A Critical Encounter*, ed. Peter McLaren and Peter Leonard (New York: Routledge, 2001), 8.

3. hooks, *Teaching to Transgress*, 185.

4. Stanley Aronowitz and Henry A. Giroux, *Postmodern Education: Politics, Culture, & Social Criticism* (Minneapolis: University of Minnesota Press, 1991), 117.

5. Stanley Aronowitz, "Paulo Freire's Radical Democratic Humanism," in *Paulo Freire: A Critical Encounter*, ed. Peter McLaren and Peter Leonard (New York: Routledge, 2001), 8.

6. Aronowitz, "Paulo Freire's Radical Democratic Humanism," 8.

7. "*Editors' Introduction*, Absent Discourses: Paulo Freire and the Dangerous Memories of Liberation" in *Paulo Freire: A Critical Encounter*, ed. Peter McLaren and Peter Leonard (New York: Routledge, 2001), 3.

8. Tomaz Tadeu da Silva and Peter McLaren, "Knowledge under Siege: The Brazilian Debate" in *Paulo Freire: A Critical Encounter*, 39.

9. Friedrich Nietzsche, *Beyond Good & Evil: Prelude to a Philosophy of the Future*, trans. Walter Kaufmann (New York: Random House, Vintage Books Edition, 1989), 11.

10. bell hooks, *Teaching Critical Thinking: Practical Wisdom* (New York: Routledge, 2010), 11.

11. See hooks, *Teaching to Transgress*, 5.

12. See Plato, Book VII of *The Republic*.

13. For instance, see Maurice Merleau-Ponty, *Phenomenology of Perception* (London: Routledge & Kegan Paul, 1962).

14. Freire, "Adult Literacy Process," 18.

15. A similar point was made by James B. Haile at the Phenomenology Roundtable in 2014. Haile emphasized how one cannot *dehistoricize concepts*. His example is that one cannot take existentialist concepts (created in a white, European, Cartesian context) and apply them unquestioningly onto an African-American context. Haile's work concerns the black existentialist writer, Thomas Slaughter.

16. Freire, "Author's Introduction," *Cultural Action for Freedom*, 7, my emphasis.

17. Freire, "Author's Introduction," *Cultural Action for Freedom*, 10.

18. Freire, "Author's Introduction," *Cultural Action for Freedom*, 11.

19. Freire, "The Adult Literacy Process," 26.

20. Freire, "The Adult Literacy Process," 31.

21. See bell hooks, "Democratic Education" in *Teaching Critical Thinking: Practical Wisdom* (New York: Routledge, 2010).

22. Judith Suissa, *Anarchism and Education: A Philosophical Perspective* (Oakland, CA: PM Press, 2010), 39.

23. Suissa, *Anarchism and Education*, 39.

24. Michael W. Apple, *Ideology and Curriculum* (New York: Routledge Falmer, 2004), xxvi.

25. Apple, *Ideology and Curriculum*, 6.

Chapter Six

Conclusion

Critical University

Why claim that critical thinking is of crucial importance? That it should be the key to higher education? I have proposed some reasons why: (1) ensuring and promoting democratic behavior and thinking, (2) helping us all to be aware of the oppression and injustice that surrounds us, (3) forming people capable of nuanced critique of systems (whether at their jobs or in the political and social realm), (4) stimulating continual ethical reflection, and (5) choosing careers and lives with an eye toward fulfillment.

Many people will claim that it is too difficult to make the changes I am suggesting; and that once settled in entrenched systems, it is hard for either an individual or organizations to get out. Giving credence to these naysayers is the idea that people behave and even *think* in habitual ways because it saves energy. Recent research suggests that this is true.[1] The individual human brain wants to save energy (to be *efficient*) and the best way to do this is through habitual thinking and behaving. While this may be true, it is also the reason why a broad liberal arts education (learning to think in many different registers) is so important. We should do our best to forge varying and diverse pathways in our brains and in the brains of others. Catherine Malabou argues that the brain is "plastic:" it is malleable and changeable throughout life. She describes the plasticity of the brain as the "synthetic alliance between the giving and receiving of form and the powerful rupture or annihilation of all form,"[2] an idea rendering the human mind radically free due to its ability "not only to passively adapt to external forces but also to actively create or destroy . . . form altogether."[3] Generally, we assume that the brain and identity are stable. Most Christian notions of the *soul* denote this kind of stability—that the soul is the heart of our identity and provides an anchor to our existence. I believe that this notion is wrong, and instead—as argued earlier—I espouse a Hegelian and Kristevian notion of the instability of the self, and indeed believe that liberation *depends* upon such instability.

Even most socialist or Marxist writers—some of those who believe in change and revolution the most!—often speak of change or revolution as if it goes in *one direction* between ideas and materiality. For instance, I have an idea, I join forces with others, and together we change the material existence of the world (for example, we fight for a living wage in our city). But the reverse is also true. Learning new philosophies, modes of art, literature, science, or languages changes the pathways that shape our brain. We shape the world, and the world also literally shapes our brains. And this shaping and reshaping of pathways goes on for our entire lives. Much of current neuroscience has studied what the brain is and how that affects our actions in the world. But likewise, how we act and learn in the world also affects our brains. Many believe that flexibility "implies only the capacity to receive form" but not to subvert it.[4] Malabou asserts, however, that "Any vision of the brain is necessarily political."[5] This gives a new and literal meaning to the phrase, "open minded."

I want to defend "instability," not just at the individual level, but also at the institutional level. Another naysayer of my work might argue that I have well defended the importance of critique and negation, but have not built a positive, stable notion of what a university must look like. I think we all ought to be suspicious of stable notions of utopia. As McLaren and da Silva point out regarding Freire's work, utopian thinking should be "provisional rather than categorical" and "to lock one's vision of the future in blue-print" is ethically dangerous.[6] As we live in a world structured by racism, sexism, and various types of oppression, any specific views we have are likely tainted. We are all affected by structural oppression, so none of our ideas are "pure" or "purely just." Recognizing this ought to provoke some care and humility. We ought to do the best thinking and critiquing that we can, knowing that our views must be open to revision and correction on the basis of justice. "A pedagogy of liberation is one that is necessarily partial and incomplete, one that has no final answers. It is always in the making, part of an ongoing struggle for critical understanding, emancipatory forms of solidarity, and the reconstitution of democratic public life."[7] We are no relativists here. As has been spelled out clearly throughout this work: there are better and worse ways of structuring the university. But we do not want to give a reductive totality to what universities must be. We must have a strategy but no final vision of a totality.

Let us now turn to my contention that critical thinking promotes lives directed toward fulfillment and ethical reflection. The work of Richard Schmitt has had a profound influence upon my own thinking on alienation in contemporary life. He argues that alienated lives do not question or seek fulfillment, although this lack of fulfillment is not solely the fault of individuals. While the possibility of individuals becoming alienated exists in any society, not all societies are *equally* alienating. Alienation includes problems of "self-identity, loneliness and a lack of meaning."[8] Schmitt refuses the "fashionable cynical stance" that insists that loneliness and lack of meaning are always "inevitable" and that those who "deny that grim fact" are "either dishonest or foolish."[9] Market society pushes people to seek individual goals and values: the more market- and commodity-based a culture becomes, the more alienation becomes commonplace among citizens. Contemporary American society "allows wide play of individual's liberty, while depriving its members of the power to make full use of these same liberties."[10] Furthermore, for most human beings, the promises of liberty are unfulfilled and they "know that they are less than they might be."[11] We are "aliens" or "exiles" from the lives we could be living if there were a different social order.[12] There is a *distance* between me and the fulfilling and passionate life that always seems just out of reach.

Schmitt asserts, and I agree, that those who are alienated do not *care* generously for others nor do they *trust* others. This brings us to another issue connected to critical thinking—that of ethical reflection. Most people have jobs in the world where they are *not able* to express their ethical beliefs, their creativity, or their passion. Nor do their jobs often give them a chance to grow and learn new skills, people, or ways of seeing—and most workers are resigned to this. Does this resignation—this sense of hopelessness—exist to this *degree* in every culture and amongst all social groups equally? Of course not. We tumble into the relativist swamp if we think that all cultures stimulate equal amounts of alienation and hopelessness. And if some cultures are less alienating than others, it behooves us as ethical persons to ask *why*. During times when unionized labor was more common amongst middle-class males in the United States, many men did bring their neighborly love and their ethical reflection to work with them.[13] I don't mean to romanticize that era: women and persons of color were not included in unionized labor to the degree that white males were. Yet, many workers of that time fought heroic and passionate battles alongside their sisters and brothers (mostly brothers!) in labor. Being union members meant extra time and effort at work, but many freely and joyously gave of it because it was a way to express deeply felt moral beliefs and care for one another. We now live in a cynical moment in which many believe that they cannot make a difference at their work or in the world. All of their love and ethical reflection are directed only to their private lives—to their families. Or perhaps to the golf course, or to shopping. This is a shame for us *all*. Most people expect to live alienated lives. They expect that their private lives will be the only place to find trust, love and meaning. They expect that their jobs will *suck*.

Marx famously stated that humans should feel *most human* while at work. Such a notion seems preposterous in this society. We have come to think that if we have a job with health insurance that pays the mortgage, we should feel "lucky" no matter what it is. That's the "best" one can hope from life. We are afraid to hope or demand more. I want to be clear that I do not blame individuals for taking or working in alienation. "The target of the theory of alienation is society."[14] This is why the major *institutions and systems* in a society bear the responsibility of working against that society's alienating tendencies. Individuals cannot fight alienation by themselves. Education—including but not limited to higher education—should be a mighty force fighting alienation in the world.

Throughout this book, I have argued that the humanities encourage our students to hope and demand more. Literature, art, history, religion, philosophy—all are ways of investigating what it means to be a human and how we can live good lives. In a good world, all humans ask these questions deeply, repeatedly, and creatively. And when we stumble across some possible answers, we need critical thinking and courage to find ways to live out those answers for and with others.

I call for *refusal*. Let us refuse to prepare students for alienated lives—to merely "train" them to make a paycheck and family and then wake up one morning and ask, how did I get here? Why does my life seem meaningless, detached and lonely? Preparing human beings for trained detachment is an expression of hatred and cynicism for students; we should want no part of it—even though such training is what passes for "realism" these days. "Despair and a sense of powerlessness" are hallmarks of alienated life.[15] This despair infects not only our students; it infects *us* when we bend ourselves to the current shape of academia without the hope or courage to change it.

My argument in this book is open to several objections, although I believe that all (or nearly all of them) fall into the camp of what is "practical" rather than what is "best." I can imagine a science professor saying that she needs grant money in order to carry out important research on cancer. I can imagine a dean of enrollment saying that my proposed changes are dangerous and might lead to a lower enrollment in the short term. I can imagine the parent of a college student saying that he fears that his child will not earn a living wage after graduating from college. I see the merit of all of these positions, given where American society is today. That is why changing higher education is not merely about paying our administrators less, having fewer adjuncts and more tenure track faculty, increasing humanities courses in general education requirements, emphasizing teaching and service more, or requiring that all university courses include critical thinking. All of these measures are necessary to turn our universities into critical spaces of inquiry. But these changes go hand-in-hand with changing our culture. We need political systems that support education rather than war. We need living wage laws. We

need free college tuition. We need health care, healthy food, safe neighbor-
hoods. We need to end the anti-intellectual biases of our culture. We need a
culture sensitive to oppression due to sex, gender, ability, race, class, and
species. We need to end the passivity of our lives so that we *all* become
activists. Changes in higher education can support these cultural and individual changes—and vice versa. Simply changing universities will not be
enough, and in fact, changing universities will not be likely unless we are
simultaneously making changes in our culture. I won't be surprised if the
number one criticism my work receives is that I'm pursuing a utopia instead
of a university. Yes. And? Why *not* build a utopia—one that is provisional,
shifting, and incomplete: always in the making? This is not an unreasonable
or unachievable ideal. We must not be frightened of the size of the task
before us. We are skeptical; but this skepticism did not grow in us without
the help of social and cultural forces. Some people benefit greatly from such
skepticism. "Critical thought and the imaginings of a better world present a
direct threat to a neoliberal paradigm in which the future replicates the
present in an endless cycle."[16] The number of people who would benefit
from these changes is large. The number of people who benefit from leaving
the system in its current state is small. Therefore, those of us who see the
problems and see ways of improving the situation must start working *today*.
Others will join the struggle when they see that their own futures are tied to
the successes of these struggles. What can you do? Commit yourself to
service and faculty governance on your college campus. Take action when
things are not right or fair. Speak up: be direct (and respectful) to your
colleagues and administration. Talk about the state of your college and specifically about adjunct pay with your students. Listen to the concerns of all
those around you. Support your adjunct union or help to form one. Be prepared to protest or strike for fair wages, transparency, ethical policies, shared
governance and critical education. Be involved in discussions about the general education requirements at your school. Be sure that every course that
students take at your university will lead them to live more fulfilling, critical
and ethical lives: accept no courses that do not. Research your own field or
area and figure out how to make your own courses more critical. Commit
yourself to building strong relationships with everyone on your campus—
students, colleagues, staff, and administration. Walk beyond the boundary of
your campus and join movements and organizations that fight for total liberation. Push your politicians to support higher education. Fight against the
instrumentalization of *education and living beings*. Start today. You will not
be alone.

NOTES

1. Contemporary neurological research explores the limits of the human mind. Recent studies have focused particularly on a mental limitation that has to do with "our ability to use a mental trait known as executive function." The brain exercises this function every time we are faced with a choice to make, (i.e., whenever conscious effort is required). It has been shown however, that employing our executive function (something we do repeatedly throughout the day even without realizing it) "draws upon a single resource of limited capacity in the brain," which means that when this resource is exhausted, our mental capacity may be "severely hindered in another, seemingly unrelated activity." Moreover, recent results suggest that "taxing mental activities," such as taking the SAT, impact not only our subsequent activities that day, as has long ago been established, but affect "the very common activity of making choices itself." From On Amir, "Thought Choices: How Making Decisions Tires Your Brain. The Brain Is Like a Muscle: When It Gets Depleted, It Becomes Less Effective," *Scientific American*, July 22, 2008, www.scientificamerican.com/article/though-choices-how-making/.

See also William B. Levy and Robert A. Baxter, "Energy-Efficient Neuronal Computation via Quantal Synaptic Failures," *The Journal of Neuroscience*, June 1, 2002, 22(11), 4746–4755.

2. Catharine Malabou, *What Should We Do with Our Brain?*, trans. by Sebastian Rand (New York: Fordham University Press, 2008), 12.

3. Hannah Proctor, "Neuronal Ideologies: Catharine Malabou's Explosive Plasticity in Light of the Marxist Psychology of A. R. Luria," *Dandelion: Postgraduate Arts Journal and Research Network*, Vol. 2, No. 1 (2011), http://dandelionjournal.org/index.php/dandelion/article/view/24/81.

4. Proctor, "Neuronal Ideologies."

5. Malabou, *What Should We Do*, 52.

We ought to pay special attention to this statement in today's society marked by a dramatic rise of what she calls "neuronal ideology," the process of adapting scientific understanding of brain plasticity to the capitalist agenda, "as though neuronal plasticity anchored biologically—and thereby justified—a certain type of political and social organization." (Malabou, *What Should We Do*, 9). It is crucial that we be aware of the remarkable power the plasticity of our brains is capable of giving us to display "disobedience to every constituted form, a refusal to submit to a model." (Malabou, *What Should We Do*, 6)

6. Peter McLaren and Tomaz Tadeu da Silva, "Decentering Pedagogy: Critical Literacy, Resistance and the Politics of Memory," in *Paulo Freire: A Critical Encounter*, ed. Peter McLaren and Peter Leonard (New York: Routledge, 2001), 69.

7. Peter McLaren and Henry A. Giroux, Ch. 1, "Radical Pedagogy as Cultural Politics: Beyond the Discourse of Critique and Anti-Utopianism," in Peter McLaren, *Critical Pedagogy and Predatory Culture: Oppositional politics in a postmodern era* (New York: Routledge, 1995), p. 57.

8. Richard Schmitt, *Alienation and Class* (Rochester, VT: Schenkman Books, Incorporated, 1983), 19.

9. Schmitt, *Alienation and Class*, 20.

10. Schmitt, *Alienation and Class*, ix.

11. Schmitt, *Alienation and Class*, ix.

12. Schmitt, *Alienation and Class*, 11.

13. Union membership density was highest in 1954 when 34.8 percent of all U.S. wage and salary workers belonged to unions; by comparison, last year only 11.3 percent of wage and salary workers were unionized. Dew Desilver, "American Unions Membership Declines as Public Support Fluctuates," *Pew Research Center*, February 20, 2014, www.pewresearch.org/fact-tank/2014/02/20/for-american-unions-membership-trails-far-behind-public-support/.

14. Richard Schmitt, *Alienation and Freedom* (Boulder, CO: Westview Press, 2002), 125.

15. Schmitt, *Alienation and Freedom*, 132.
16. Giroux, *Neoliberalism's War on Higher Education*, 31.

Bibliography

Alexander, Jacqui M. *Pedagogies of Crossing: Meditiations on Feminism, Sexual Politics, Memory, and the Sacred.* Durham, NC: Duke University Press, 2005.

Althusser, Louis. *Lenin and Philosophy and Other Essays.* Translated by Ben Brewster. New York: Monthly Review Press, 2001.

———. *On Ideology.* New York: Verso Books, 2008.

Althusser, Loius, and Étienne Balibar. *Reading Capital.* Translated by Ben Brestwer. New York: Verso Books, 2009.

Amir, On. "Thought Choices: How Making Decisions Tires Your Brain. The Brain Is Like a Muscle: When It Gets Depleted, It Becomes Less Effective." *Scientific American.* July 22, 2008. www.scientificamerican.com/article/though-choices-how-making/.

Apple, Michael W. *Ideology and Curriculum.* New York: RoutledgeFalmer, 2004.

Arendt, Hannah. *Eichmann in Jerusalem: A Report on the Banality of Evil.* New York: The Viking Press, Inc., 1963.

Aronowitz, Stanley, and Henry A. Giroux. *Postmodern Education: Politics, Culture, & Social Criticism.* Minneapolis: University of Minnesota Press, 1991.

At Berkeley. Directed by Frederick Wiseman. USA, 2013. DVD.

Baez, Benjamin, and Deron Boyles. *The Politics of Inquiry: Education Research and the "Culture of Science."* Albany: State University of New York Press, 2009.

Beauvoir, Simone de. *The Ethics of Ambiguity.* Translated by Bernard Frechtman. New York: The Citadel Press, 1964.

Beercroft, Alex. "Defenses of the Humanities: The Two Cultures." *A New Deal for the Humanities* (blog). January 25, 2014. http://newdealhumanities.com/2014/01/25/defenses-of-the-humanities-the-two-cultures/.

Bennett, Brian. "NCAA Board Votes to Allow Autonomy." *ESPN College Sports.* August 8, 2014. http://espn.go.com/college-sports/story/_/id/11321551/ncaa-board-votes-allow-autonomy-five-power-conferences.

Best, Steven, and Douglas Kellner. "Postmodern Politics and the Battle for the Future," in *Illuminations* (2002). www.uta.edu/huma/illuminations/kell28.htm.

Bok, Derek. *Universities in the Marketplace: The Commercialization of Higher Education.* Princeton, NJ: Princeton University Press, 2003.

Canisius College. *News and Events.* http://www.canisius.edu/newsevents/.

Caputo, John D. "Jacques Derrida (1930–2004)." *Journal for Cultural and Religious Theory,* Vol. 6, No. 1 (December 2004): 6–9. www.jcrt.org/archives/06.1/caputo.pdf.

Chokshi, Niraj. "Vermont Just Passed the Nation's First GMO Food Labeling Law. Now it Prepares to Get Sued." *The Washington Post.* May 9, 2014. www.washingtonpost.com/blogs/govbeat/wp/2014/04/29/how-vermont-plans-to-defend-the-nations-first-gmo-law/.

Chomsky, Noam. "How America's Great University System Is Being Destroyed." *AlterNet.* February 28, 2014. www.alternet.org/corporate-accountability-and-workplace/chomsky-how-americas-great-university-system-getting?paging=off&current_page=1#bookmark.

Committee on Labor Relations, American Anthropological Association. *Resolution on Contingent & Part-time Academic Labor.* November 21, 2013. http://sunta.org/files/2010/12/Resolution-on-Contingent-Part-time-Academic-Labor.-.pdf.

Delta Cost Project at American Institutes for Research. "Labor Intensive or Labor Expensive?" February 2014. www.deltacostproject.org/sites/default/files/products/DeltaCostAIR_Staffing_Brief_2_3_14.pdf.

Derrida, Jacques. "The Principle of Reason" in *Eyes of the University: Right to Philosophy 2.* Edited by Werner Hamacher and David E. Wellbery. Translated by Jan Plug and Others. Stanford, CA: Stanford University Press, 2004.

Desilver, Dew. "American Unions Membership Declines as Public Support Fluctuates." *Pew Research Center.* February 20, 2014. www.pewresearch.org/fact-tank/2014/02/20/for-american-unions-membership-trails-far-behind-public-support/.

Digest of Education Statistics, published by the National Center for Education Statistics. http://nces.ed.gov/.

Durisin, Megan, and Jeff Wilson. "U.S. Grain Losses Seen Up to $6.3 Billion on China Ban." *Bloomberg.* April 16, 2014. http://www.bloomberg.com/news/articles/2014-04-16/u-s-group-says-losses-may-be-6-3-billion-on-china-corn.

Eagleton, Terry. *Ideology: An Introduction.* New York: Verso Books, 2007.

Earthlings. Directed by Shaun Monson. 2005. Nation Earth, 2008. DVD.

Fish, Stanley. "The Crisis of the Humanities Officially Arrives." *New York Times.* October 11, 2010. http://opinionator.blogs.nytimes.com/2010/10/11/the-crisis-of-the-humanities-officially-arrives/?_php=true&_type=blogs&_r=0.

Freire, Paulo. *Cultural Action for Freedom.* Cambridge, MA: Harvard Educational Review and the Center for the Study of Development and Social Change, 2000.

Freud, Sigmund. *Civilization and Its Discontents.* Translated and Edited by James Strachey. New York: W. W. Norton & Company, 1961/1930.

"Gently Modified." *The Economist.* January 17, 2015, www.economist.com/news/europe/21639578-eu-lifts-its-ban-gm-crops-gently-modified.

Gerber, Larry G. *The Rise and Decline of Faculty Governance: Professionalization and the Modern American University.* Baltimore: Johns Hopkins University Press, 2014.

Ginsberg, Benjamin. "Administrators Ate My Tuition." *Washington Monthly.* September/October 2011. www.washingtonmonthly.com/magazine/septemberoctober_2011/features/administrators_ate_my_tuition031641.php?page=all#.

Giroux, Henry A. *Neoliberalism's War on Higher Education.* Chicago: Haymarket Books, 2014.

———. *Theory and Resistance in Education.* Westport, CT: Bergin & Garvey, 2001.

Gordon, Lewis. R. "Manifesto of Transdisciplinarity. Not to Become Slaves of the Knowledge of Others." *Trans-pasando Fronteras,* No 1 (2011). www.icesi.edu.co/revistas/index.php/trans-pasando_fronteras/rt/printerFriendly/1289/1755.

Greene, Jay P., Brian Kisida, and Jonathan Mills. "Administrative Bloat at American Universities: The Real Reason for High Costs in Higher Education." *Goldwater Institute Policy Report,* No. 239, August 17, 2010. http://goldwaterinstitute.org/sites/default/files/Administrative%20Bloat.pdf.

Hart, James G. "The Essential Look (*Eidos*) of the Humanities: A Husserlian Phenomenology of the University." *Tijdschrift voor Filosofie* (70/ 2008, 109–139).

Heidegger, Martin. *Being and Time.* Translated by John Macquarrie and Edward Robinson. Oxford: Basil Blackwell, 1962/1927.

Hersch, Richard H., and John Merrow, eds. *Declining by Degrees: Higher Education at Risk.* New York: Palgrave MacMillan, 2006.

hooks, bell. *Teaching Critical Thinking: Practical Wisdom.* New York: Routledge, 2010.

———. *Teaching to Transgress: Education as the Practice of Freedom.* New York: Routledge, 1994.

Jameson, Fredric. *Postmodernism or the Cultural Logic of Late Capitalism.* Durham, NC: Duke University Press, 1991.

Jaschik, Scott. "Big Union Win." *Inside Higher Ed.* January 2, 2015, www.insidehighered.com/news/2015/01/02/nlrb-ruling-shifts-legal-ground-faculty-unions-private-colleges.

June, Audrey Williams, and Jonah Newman. "Adjunct Project Reveals Wide Range in Pay." *The Chronicle of Higher Education.* January 4, 2013. http://chronicle.com/article/Adjunct_Pay_Conditions/136439/.

Kerl, Eric. "Contemporary Anarchism." *International Socialist Review*, Issue # 72, July 2010.

Kristeva, Julia. *Intimate Revolt: The Powers and Limits of Psychoanalysis, Volume 2.* Translated by Jeanine Herman. New York: Columbia University Press, 2002/1997.

———. *The Sense and Non-Sense of Revolt: The Powers and Limits of Psychoanalysis, Volume 1.* Translated by Jeanine Herman. New York: Columbia University Press, 2000/1996.

Krznaric, Roman. *How to Find Fulfilling Work.* The School of Life 2012, Macmillan.

LaBarber, Jourdon. "Retirement Buyouts Aim to Minimize Faculty Layoffs." *The Griffin.* April 25. 2014. http://canisiusgriffin.com/?p=7430.

Lee, Jaeah, and Maggie Severns. "Charts: When College Presidents Are Paid Like CEOs." *Mother Jones.* September 5, 2013. www.motherjones.com/politics/2013/09/charts-college-presidents-overpaid-pay.

Levy, William B., and Robert A. Baxter. "Energy-Efficient Neuronal Computation via Quantal Synaptic Failures." *The Journal of Neuroscience.* 22(11), 4746–4755.

Malabou, Catherine. *What Should We Do with Our Brain?* Translated by Sebastian Rand. New York: Fordham University Press, 2008.

Marcus, Jon. "New Analysis Shows Problematic Boom in Higher Ed Administrators." *Huffington Post.* February 6, 2014. www.huffingtonpost.com/2014/02/06/higher-ed-administrators-growth_n_4738584.html.

Marcuse, Herbert. *The Aesthetic Dimension: Toward a Critique of Marxist Aesthetics.* Translated by Herbert Marcuse and Erica Sherover. Boston: Beacon Press, 1978.

———. *Eros and Civilization: A Philosophical Inquiry into Freud.* Boston: Beacon Press, 1966/1955.

Martin, Robert E. "College Costs Too Much Because Faculty Lack Power." *The Chronicle of Higher Education.* August 5, 2012. http://chronicle.com/article/College-Costs-Too-Much-Because/133357/.

Martin, Robert E., and R. Carter Hill. "Baumol and Bowen Cost Effects in Research Universities." September 2012. wwu.edu/provost/communication/documents/BenchmarkReport_FacultytoAdminRatio.pdf.

McLaren, Peter. *Critical Pedagogy and Predatory Culture: Oppositional Politics in a Postmodern Era.* New York: Routledge, 1995.

McLaren, Peter, and Peter Leonard, eds. *Paulo Freire: A Critical Encounter.* New York: Routledge, 2001.

McPhie, Neil A. G., et al. "As Supervisors Retire: An Opportunity to Reshape Organizations. A Report to the President and the Congress of the United States by the U.S. Merit Systems Protection Board." October 2009. www.mspb.gov/netsearch/viewdocs.aspx?docnumber=457394&version=458606.

"Monsanto-Killer or 'Trojan Horse'? New Law Lets EU States Ban GM Crops." *RT News*, December 5, 2014. http://rt.com/news/211811-eu-gm-monsanto-trojan/.

Newman, Jonah. "Highest-Paid Presidents Face Backlash, Study Finds." *The Chronicle of Higher Education.* December 15, 2013. http://chronicle.com/article/Highest-Paid-Presidents-Face/143599/.

Nietzsche, Friedrich. *Beyond Good & Evil: Prelude to a Philosophy of the Future.* Translated by Walter Kaufmann. New York: Random House, Vintage Books Edition, 1989.

Nocella, Anthony J., II, Steven Best, and Peter McLaren, eds. *Academic Repression: Reflections from the Academic Industrial Complex.* Oakland: AK Press, 2010.

Nussbaum, Martha. *Not For Profit: Why Democracy Needs the Humanities.* Princeton, NJ: Princeton University Press, 2010.

Obama, Barack. "Remarks by the President and Dr. Jill Biden at White House Summit on Community Colleges." The White House: Office of the Press Secretary. October 5, 2010. www.whitehouse.gov/the-press-office/2010/10/05/remarks-president-and-dr-jill-biden-white-house-summit-community-college.

———. "Remarks by the President on College Affordability, Syracuse, NY." The White House: Office of the Press Secretary. August 22, 2013. www.whitehouse.gov/the-press-office/2013/08/23/remarks-president-college-affordability-syracuse-ny.

Peter, Josh, and Steve Berkowitz. "Special Report: Coaches Hit Jackpot in NCAA System." *USA TODAY Sports*. April 2, 2014. www.usatoday.com/story/sports/ncaab/2014/04/02/ncaa-tournament-basketball-coaches-compensation-obannon-case/7208877/.

Plato. *The Republic*. Translated by G. M. A. Grube. Revised by C. D. C. Reeve. 2nd Edition. Indianapolis: Hackett Publishing Company, 1992.

Proctor, Hannah. "Neuronal Ideologies: Catharine Malabou's Explosive Plasticity in Light of the Marxist Psychology of A. R. Luria." *Dandelion: Postgraduate Arts Journal and Research Network*, Vol. 2, No. 1 (2011). http://dandelionjournal.org/index.php/dandelion/article/view/24/81.

Reitz, Charles. *Art, Alienation and the Humanities: A Critical Engagement with Herbert Marcuse*. New York: State University of New York Press, 2000.

Reitz, Charles. Crisis and Commonwealth: Marcuse, Marx, McLaren. Lanham, MD: Lexington Books, 2013.

Ricoeur, Paul. *Freud and Philosophy: An Essay on Interpretation*. Translated by Denis Savage. New Haven: Yale University Press, 1970/1965.

Rogers, Jenny. "3 to 1: That's the Best Ratio of Tenure-Track Faculty to Administrators, a Study Concludes." *The Chronicle of Higher Education*. November 1, 2012. http://chronicle.com/article/Administrative-Bloat-How-Much/135500/.

Rooney, Ellen. "Better Read Than Dead: Althusser and the Fetish of Ideology." *Yale French Studies*, No. 88 (1995).

Rosovsky, Henry. *The University: An Owner's Manual*. New York: W. W. Norton & Company, 1991.

"Salary Increase By Major." *The Wall Street Journal*. http://online.wsj.com/public/resources/documents/info-Degrees_that_Pay_you_Back-sort.html.

Sandel, Michael. *What Money Can't Buy: The Moral Limits of Markets*. New York: Farrar, Straus and Giroux, 2012.

Schmitt, Richard. *Alienation and Class*. Vermont: Schenkman Books, Incorporated, 1983.

———. *Alienation and Freedom*. Boulder, CO: Westview Press, 2002.

Schuman, Rebecca. "Student Evaluations of Professors Aren't Just Biased and Absurd–They Don't Even Work." *Slate*. April 24, 2014. www.slate.com/articles/life/education/2014/04/student_evaluations_of_college_professors_are_biased_and_worthless.html.

Stark, Philip. "Do Student Evaluations Measure Teaching Effectiveness?" *The Berkeley Blog*. October 14, 2013. http://blogs.berkeley.edu/2013/10/14/do-student-evaluations-measure-teaching-effectiveness/.

Stripling, Jack, and Jonah Newman. "4 Public-College Presidents Pass $1-Million Mark in Pay." *The Chronicle of Higher Education*. May 12, 2013. http://chronicle.com/article/4-Public-College-Chiefs-Pass/139189/.

Suissa, Judith. *Anarchism and Education: A Philosophical Perspective*. Oakland: PM Press, 2010.

The Future of Food. Directed by Deborah Koons Garcia. USA: Lily Films, 2004. DVD.

The Pervert's Guide to Ideology. Directed by Sophie Fiennes. 2012. United Kingdom, 2013. DVD.

They Live! Directed by John Carpenter. 1988. USA, 2003. DVD.

Tokasz, Jay. "Erie Community College creates new position despite revenue shortfalls." *The Buffalo News*. June 26, 2014. www.buffalonews.com/city-region/erie-community-college/erie-community-college-creates-new-position-despite-revenue-shortfalls-20140626.

"Too Many Managers?" *SEIU Local 503*. April 7, 2011. www.seiu503.org/2011/04/too-many-managers/.

U.S. Supreme Court. *National Labor Relations Board v. Yeshiva University*, No. 78-857. Argued October 10, 1979, decided February 20, 1980. 444 U.S. 672. http://supreme.justia. com/cases/federal/us/444/672/.

Young, Iris Marion. *Justice and the Politics of Difference*. Princeton, NJ: Princeton University Press, 1990.

Index